One flesh

Marriage as God Intended

Henry and Michele Buford

Acknowledgements

~ First and foremost, we thank God almighty for giving us the opportunity to praise and worship Him through the writing of this book

~ To all our brothers and sisters in Christ that challenged us to seek God's wisdom on how to be one flesh in our marriage.

~ To Jonathan and Jessica for sacrificing their time with us to write this book.

~ To our parents for being just that...our parents.

~ And to all our family and friends for their support, even when they had no idea we were writing this book.

Contents

Introduction

Over the years, my wife and I have been members of numerous non-denominational churches in North Carolina, Florida, Wisconsin and Pennsylvania. In our walk with Christ we have, on numerous occasions, led ministries as unpaid lay members of our churches. It is our firm conviction that every church needs to have at least one or two "right hand" couples that share the burden of leadership so the work of every leader may be a joy.

As we have matured in our walk with God, we have encountered numerous challenges and struggles. Some of these struggles are captured here in this book. Still, we have many more challenges that are awaiting another opportunity for sharing. God has granted us these refining challenges because He loves us and wants for us to become more useful in His kingdom.

Over time, we have noticed that many people have commented on the strength of our marriage. While many people have made this observation, we often find it difficult to articulate, in just a few words, how God has been able to do the things that He has done in our lives. We have spent several years discussing and talking about writing this book before any words arrived on paper.

This book is intended to be a tool that can be used in ministry capacities to build up God's kingdom. It should be noted that this book has been written by a couple with little or no formal ministry training. We are regular people just like everybody else. We are not "Super Christians" as if there were such a thing, but rather people that balance working jobs, while studying the Bible with people and teaching them the good news about Jesus. In this book we talk about principles and actions that we live by everyday because they are attainable by everyone that relies, not on their own strength, but on the power of God.

How many pennies are in a penny anyway?

One flesh

A marriage occurs when two people become one. They are one in thought, deed, desire, compassion, and life. If one member in the marriage has a thought or desire, so the other member of the marriage has this same thought and desire. When one is compassionate, the other is compassionate as well. A marriage is the sharing of a single life. This oneness is an immutable fact. In much the same way as gravity, failure to believe in this fact does not remove the consequences of ignoring it.

Many marriages suffer because they have never been taught how to live in accordance with this law that God has provided for us. To some degree, this has been influenced greatly by popular cultural beliefs that each individual is the sole controller of his or her destiny and that marriage does not in any way alter this egocentric drive. This perception is entirely devoid of scriptural support and as such can be described only as "worldly wisdom" with which your mileage will vary. As we examine the scriptures, we will see that God has worked out a marvelous plan for marriage that is extremely fulfilling when we live in accordance with this law of unity that He designed.

Oddly enough, not only has this concept been foreign to the world, but it also seems to have eluded many a church. Perhaps the math is more complicated than it seems on the surface. This leads us to offer a simple analogy to help us put this into perspective, how many pennies are in a penny? In Genesis 2, marriage is defined thusly:

> **21** So the LORD God caused the man to fall into a deep sleep; and while he was sleeping, he took one of the man's ribs and then closed up the place with flesh. **22** Then the LORD God made a woman from the rib he had taken out of the man, and he brought her to the man. **23** The man said, "This is now bone of my bones and flesh of my flesh; she shall be called 'woman,' for she was taken out of man." **24** That is why a man leaves his father and mother and is united to his wife, and they become one flesh. **25** Adam and his wife were both naked, and they felt no shame. **NIV**

We should start our observation of marriage by understanding what it is and what it is not. Marriage is a relationship in which two people are one. We can infer therefore, that anything that does not look like this is not a marriage. Perhaps it may be a relationship of convenience, but it would not be a marriage if the two do not think and act as one.

One flesh

Man and woman are meant for intimacy with one another. In this scripture, we see Adam and his wife were not ashamed to be naked together. This kind of intimacy is perfectly normal in a marital relationship and should be found in every marriage.

From this passage, we can see that woman was created from an inner part of man, not of his choosing or will, but at the will of God. In many cultures, there exists a freedom of individuals to choose for themselves a spouse whom they may marry. At times, we can allow for this freedom to make us feel as though God is not working through our choice of relationships. The reality is that God has created this spouse for you, perhaps before He even created you. Those of us for whom God has prepared marriage, our interconnecting paths have been laid out, so that we can be fulfilled to the depths of our innermost being based upon the design and plan that God has laid out for us in our lives. King David wrote about this plan in Psalm 139:13-16:

> [13] For you created my inmost being; you knit me together in my mother's womb. [14] I praise you because I am fearfully and wonderfully made; your works are wonderful, I know that full well. [15] My frame was not hidden from you when I was made in the secret place, when I was woven together

> in the depths of the earth. [16] Your
> eyes saw my unformed body; all
> the days ordained for me were
> written in your book before one of
> them came to be.   **NIV**

Even before we saw the light of our very first day on this earth, God had ordained for us His plan. God wrote in His book everything that He carefully laid out for us. He created not only our innermost being, but everything that would provide us with the fulfillment we all desire and need. No one knows what we need quite as well as our Creator. He freely makes beautiful plans for our lives so that we can be filled with His blessings of love and joy.

God has plans for every man, woman, and child that seeks to have a relationship with Him. This has always been a part of God's nature. In Jeremiah 29:11-14, we find a promise that God gave to the Israelites:

> [11] For I know the plans I have for
> you," declares the LORD, "plans to
> prosper you and not to harm you,
> plans to give you hope and a
> future. [12] Then you will call on me
> and come and pray to me, and I
> will listen to you. [13] You will seek
> me and find me when you seek me
> with all your heart. [14] I will be
> found by you," declares the LORD,

> "and will bring you back from
> captivity. I will gather you from all
> the nations and places where I
> have banished you," declares the
> LORD, "and will bring you back to
> the place from which I carried you
> into exile."   **NIV**

This promise was given to the Israelites because God had a very specific plan for each and every one of them just as He has a specific plan for each one of us. Selfishly, we often fail to notice that God's plan for us is conditional. It comes with the condition that if we seek God with all of our hearts, He will be found by us. God very much desires to have a relationship with His people, but this is not possible if we are unwilling to seek after our creator. God is imploring us in this scripture to seek after Him with all of our hearts. All of our inmost being must participate in this search for our creator in order for us to be brought back from the captivity in which He has banished us. It will be then and only then that we will truly be able to find God and His plans to prosper us in our lives here on earth.

Often times, the conditional nature of God's promises confuses and frustrates people who are determined to maintain a perception of their own self importance. In much the same way as this conditional promise, God's free gift of eternal life is available to all mankind under the condition that we seek a relationship with Jesus with all of our hearts. God's gifts are free, but it is up to each individual person to seek out God's requirements in order for them to reach out and partake of these gifts.

Shamefully, some spouses assert disparaging terms against each other. The oneness of marriage creates an environment in which this has the effect of the childhood saying "I'm rubber and you're glue; whatever you say bounces off of me and sticks to you." In a marriage, it is not possible to disparage your spouse without at the same time disparaging yourself. This is true on every level of analysis. Is your spouse a fool? Obviously, you would be a fool also because you chose to marry them.

It is important to understand and appreciate the character flaws in your spouse. God has given you the ability to see them not to empower you to disparage your spouse, but to enable you to help yourself since you and your spouse are one. In helping yourself you should be careful not to perform surgery on yourself when you are angry with yourself, untrained, or simply unqualified to perform the task. This is certainly an area where a bevy of legitimate experience is helpful. If your left hand is struggling with alcoholism and your right hand has never touched a drink or ever even known a drunk, pop-culture psychology is not a good way to help your left hand. There may be more cases than immediately thought where it is

7

more helpful to seek advice or assistance before attempting self-surgery.

Modern culture teaches us a sense of 'individualism' that is often wrought with an advocacy of schizophrenic marriages. There is no reason for a married man and woman to be intimately close to one another and be ashamed of his or her behavior. Marriage is actually made strong when husband and wife communicate on deep and intimate levels. This requires both frequent and specific communication from both members of the union. Failure to stay in consistent communication leads to 'split-brain' behavior where part of the body is unaware of the actions and desires of the other and consequently causes significant damage to the body regardless of whether or not the body recognizes or addresses the wounds that get inflicted under these conditions.

Even before modern times, divorce of convenience has been attempted and achieved on many occasions. In fact, the first divorce in the Bible is attempted very shortly after the first marriage. Adam attempts to separate himself from his wife immediately upon realizing that he has sinned.

Genesis 3:11-12:

> [11] And he said, "Who told you that you were naked? Have you eaten

> from the tree that I commanded
> you not to eat from?" **12** The man
> said, "The woman you put here
> with me—she gave me some fruit
> from the tree, and I ate it." **NIV**

In this passage, Adam presents his case before God as if he
is innocent of any wrongdoing. Before stepping too far off
into what constitutes a marriage, let us take a look at how
God defines oneness. For example, God's Church is one
body 1 Corinthians 12:12-31

> **12** Just as a body, though one, has
> many parts, but all its many parts
> form one body, so it is with Christ.
> **13** For we were all baptized by one
> Spirit so as to form one body—
> whether Jews or Gentiles, slave or
> free—and we were all given the
> one Spirit to drink. **14** Even so the
> body is not made up of one part
> but of many. **15** Now if the foot
> should say, "Because I am not a
> hand, I do not belong to the body,"
> it would not for that reason stop
> being part of the body. **16** And if
> the ear should say, "Because I am
> not an eye, I do not belong to the
> body," it would not for that reason
> stop being part of the body. **17** If
> the whole body were an eye, where
> would the sense of hearing be? If

the whole body were an ear, where would the sense of smell be? [18] But in fact God has placed the parts in the body, every one of them, just as he wanted them to be. [19] If they were all one part, where would the body be? [20] As it is, there are many parts, but one body. [21] The eye cannot say to the hand, "I don't need you!" And the head cannot say to the feet, "I don't need you!" [22] On the contrary, those parts of the body that seem to be weaker are indispensable, [23] and the parts that we think are less honorable we treat with special honor. And the parts that are unpresentable are treated with special modesty, [24] while our presentable parts need no special treatment. But God has put the body together, giving greater honor to the parts that lacked it, [25] so that there should be no division in the body, but that its parts should have equal concern for each other. [26] If one part suffers, every part suffers with it; if one part is honored, every part rejoices with it. [27] Now you are the body of Christ, and each one of you is a part of it. [28] And God has placed in the church first of all

> apostles, second prophets, third
> teachers, then miracles, then gifts
> of healing, of helping, of guidance,
> and of different kinds of tongues.
> [29] Are all apostles? Are all
> prophets? Are all teachers? Do all
> work miracles? [30] Do all have gifts
> of healing? Do all speak in
> tongues? Do all interpret? [31] Now
> eagerly desire the greater gifts.
>
> **NIV**

Like the Church, a marriage is made of multiple parts.
Specifically, there are two parts in a marriage – Husband
and Wife. These parts come together in a union that binds
them and holds them steadfast before God and man.
Although one part of the body may be more useful than
the other, both parts are required in order to form the one
body.

Now let us return back to Adam and consider what
he attempted before God to do with Eve, his wife. Adam
has proclaimed that his hand (Eve) gave him the fruit and
he ate of it. However, in his context and tone, he
proposed the idea that his wife was somehow separate
from him. Allegedly, he felt as though he had achieved a
sort of individualism that is not in step with God's
definition of marriage. By God's definition, Adam and Eve
are "one flesh." If they are one flesh, then it cannot be
possible for there to be two individuals. There is no room

for two pennies inside one penny. Pop culture would teach us otherwise, but in reality, one is a singular number, indivisible, and indispensible.

The oneness of marriage has been under attack since the beginning of time. As you can see from the example of Adam, man has tried to separate himself from his wife at almost every time it becomes convenient for him to be single. To his shame, he has cast off his wife because he deemed it more beneficial for him to be alone than to be married. He incorrectly believed that he and his wife were somehow separate entities, despite the obvious fact that they were bound together as one flesh from the creation of time. At times, we too fail to see that our spouses are an extension of ourselves. When we do this we are divorcing ourselves from our spouses. We are creating an ungodly separation that God never meant or sanctioned. Malachi 2:16 demonstrates how God feels about this behavior:

> **16** "I hate divorce," says the
> LORD, the God of Israel, "because
> the man who divorces his wife
> covers his garment with violence,"
> **NIV**

Failing to recognize and acknowledge our spouse as part of our own flesh is sin. God hates this behavior and it is not appropriate for any of God's children.

In many cultures across the world, divorce is a very commonly accepted practice that permeates all levels of socioeconomics and status. Clearly, God never meant for this to be the case. Ironically, despite this admonition and condemnation of the practice, many Christian churches not only condone divorce, but also advocate it as a panacea that quickly resolves the minor inconveniences that may occur within a marriage. If God hates divorce, how much more should a Christian hate it? How does the Christian that advocates divorce reconcile this scripture with their doctrine? This advocacy cannot exist within the Christian community for several reasons. In modern times, divorce has become a matter of legality. The dissolution of marriage now requires legal proceedings and actually demonstrates that the divorcing parties are, in fact, not Christians at all. In 1 Corinthians 6:1-7, Paul writes about how marital disputes should be settled within the church:

> [1] If any of you has a dispute with another, do you dare to take it before the ungodly for judgment instead of before the Lord's people? [2] Or do you not know that the Lord's people will judge the world? And if you are to judge the world, are you not competent to judge trivial cases? [3] Do you not know that we will judge angels? How much more the things of this

> life! **4** Therefore, if you have
> disputes about such matters, do
> you ask for a ruling from those
> whose way of life is scorned in the
> church? **5** I say this to shame you.
> Is it possible that there is nobody
> among you wise enough to judge a
> dispute between believers? **6** But
> instead, one brother takes another
> to court—and this in front of
> unbelievers! **7** The very fact that
> you have lawsuits among you
> means you have been completely
> defeated already. Why not rather
> be wronged? Why not rather be
> cheated?   **NIV**

This scripture makes it clear that at least one party in the marriage must not be a Christian in order for a divorce to be possible, because if both spouses are Christians, they are also a brother and a sister in the church with a dispute between them. In humility, the Christian would rather be wronged than take their dispute to court to determine justice for themselves. This scripture illustrates that lawsuits among believers indicates their Christianity has been completely defeated already.

The oneness of marriage begins with commitment. On the day that we got married our vows read as, "I _____, take you _____, to be my wedded wife/husband. To have and to hold, from this day forward, for better, for worse, for richer, for poorer, in sickness or in health, to love and to cherish 'till death do us part. And hereto I pledge you my faithfulness" (myweddingvows.com, 2004). True commitment means seriously contemplating the question "what if my life is forever worse, with less money, or an incurable illness if I marry this person?" Most people are either unable or unwilling to consider these possibilities. Unfortunately, a reality that we must all face is that marriage will not necessarily make our lives intrinsically better in humanly measurable ways. The decision to marry is less about what you will get out of marriage than what you desire to give to someone else in marriage. Marriage is a selfless act.

Over time, this selfless act has been commonly attempted by selfish people who neither understand the unselfish nature of the marriage commitment, nor do they value the character building that results from the suffering they incur when placing the interests of their spouse ahead of their own. In many regions of the world, the selfish so-called 'marriages' outnumber the unselfish sacrificing marriages and cause people confusion in regard to what a marriage should really look like. Marriage is not be used as a license for sex, as it is used in many Muslim communities to justify prostitution. It is rightly so that many Muslims condemn this practice of 'one-day' marriage for the purpose of legal sexual intercourse as it only pretends to obey the letter of the law. This practice fails to even begin to account for how God feels about divorce.

Any credible examination of the marital bond shows us that it is exceptionally strong and intimately close. Marriage should be entered upon with trepidation. When asked about marriage, Jesus tried to impress this upon His hearers so that they might respect the sanctity of marriage. Matthew 19:3-11 reads:

> [3] Some Pharisees came to him to test him. They asked, "Is it lawful for a man to divorce his wife for any and every reason?" [4] "Haven't you read," he replied, "that at the beginning the Creator 'made them male and female,' [5] and said, 'For this reason a man will leave his father and mother and be united to his wife, and the two will become one flesh'? [6] So they are no longer two, but one flesh. Therefore what God has joined together, let no one separate." [7] "Why then," they asked, "did Moses command that a man give his wife a certificate of divorce and send her away?" [8] Jesus replied, "Moses permitted you to divorce your wives because your hearts were hard. But it was not this way from the beginning. [9] I tell you that anyone who divorces

> his wife, except for sexual
> immorality, and marries another
> woman commits adultery." [10] The
> disciples said to him, "If this is the
> situation between a husband and
> wife, it is better not to marry." [11]
> Jesus replied, "Not everyone can
> accept this word, but only those to
> whom it has been given.   **NIV**

Truthfully, taking marriage lightly is not a new, regional, or cultural problem. This problem has existed throughout the ages. Jesus addresses it specifically in these scriptures to illustrate that the "hard hearts" of selfish men and women have created the institution of divorce. Thousands of years ago, marriage was being taken lightly. It has been viewed repeatedly as an avenue to sexual pleasure, a way to appease a desired mate, an obligation to meet the approval of parents, and even a means to citizenship in a country of choice. The abuse of the marriage rite has even at times caused people to question its legitimacy. Under these misguided views of what constitutes a marriage, virtually any relationship of two or more people could be construed as being a marriage. In some cultures, marriage has taken legal forms that clearly are not similar or related to what is defined in the Bible.

Marriage has been abused for centuries. However, the institution itself has not for that reason become illegitimate. This notion is as if to say that because there are lawbreaking fugitives living amongst law abiding citizens then it is reasonable to assume that people are lawbreakers. Even if it is difficult to determine one type of person from another, they would not all for that reason become one and the same. Divorce is an outgrowth of the abuse of marriage. A more appropriate view of what marriage is and what it is intended to be is necessary to help people make better judgments for marital commitment.

In this passage of scripture in Matthew, Jesus differentiates God's plan from what God is willing to allow or tolerate among His people. Jesus points out to them that God has made them one flesh, but because men's hearts were hard, God gave them grace by means of divorce even though this was never part of God's plan. As Jesus has described it here, divorce is only tolerated by God because of the sin and hardness of men's hearts.

It seems to be rather clear that the apostle Paul had made a calculated decision not to involve himself in marriage. This should be seen as an indication of how serious this commitment should be and that it should not be taken lightly, as it is not meant to be for everyone. Paul goes so far as to write about marriage in 1 Corinthians 7:25-28:

> [25] Now about virgins: I have no command from the Lord, but I give

a judgment as one who by the
Lord's mercy is trustworthy. **26**
Because of the present crisis, I
think that it is good for a man to
remain as he is. **27** Are you pledged
to a woman? Do not seek to be
released. Are you free from such a
commitment? Do not look for a
wife. **28** But if you do marry, you
have not sinned; and if a virgin
marries, she has not sinned. But
those who marry will face many
troubles in this life, and I want to
spare you this.   **NIV**

Paul makes the point here that if you choose to marry, you
will necessarily face many troubles in your life. This is not
exactly the rosy picture that we see in magazines, movies,
or television shows. Clearly it is not sinful to engage in
marriage, but there will be many trials and a decision not
to marry may be an honest and realistic decision. Paul's
desire here is to spare us of the troubles in life that will
befall all of those that choose to marry.

Modern society has nearly universally taken the
position that marriage is an inalienable right that has been
bequeathed to all mankind. Surely, Jesus does not
espouse this belief nor does He suggest that in this
passage. When Jesus says that not everyone can accept
this word, He is making it clear that marriage is not for
everyone and that it should be treated with the utmost

respect. Marriage requires a commitment that can only be rivaled by your commitment to God Himself. In many ways, your commitment to your spouse is part of your commitment to God.

The over glamorization of marriage has clouded the judgment of many people who think that marriage is an avenue for personal gain. If anything, marriage is a path to suffering and troubles as Paul has described in 1 Corinthians 7 and Christians should seriously consider a life being spared of this. While marriage can be very rewarding and fulfilling, it can never be either of these without troubles or exceedingly great sacrifice. If marriage is not approached without a sincere understanding of the commitment, suffering, persecution, and sacrifice required to have a rewarding and fulfilling marriage, then the couple considering marriage should seriously consider what their alternatives might be.

All over the world, marriage is treated more like a right than a privilege. The consequence for failing to grasp or appreciate the oneness of marriage manifests itself in rampant divorce as people shed spouses like yesterday's clothing. A penny is not meant to be split apart. When you split a penny, you make it worth less than nothing. Rejoining the separated parts requires a far greater expenditure of energy than keeping them together in the first place. Adjoining each separate part to other parts in

the futile hope of creating a meaningful unit is like trying
to stop the rain with your hands. There is no shortage of
studies that demonstrate that second marriages have
higher divorce rates than first marriages, in part because
once a heart decides that marriage is not truly meant to be
one flesh, shedding a second marriage comes more easily
than shedding the first. In some cases, a second divorce
seems only natural to those who partake in them.

One is not a number that is meant to be
fractionalized in the fulfillment of God's plan for marriage.
While God is certainly patient and willing to help us along
our journeys, the oneness of marriage has no examples of
advocated separation or division within the Bible. Jesus
gives us an example of when a marriage "can" be
separated, but He does not argue that the marriage must
be separated. We find Jesus' example of when divorce can
be tolerated in Matthew 5:31-32:

> [31] "It has been said, 'Anyone who
> divorces his wife must give her a
> certificate of divorce.' [32] But I tell
> you that anyone who divorces his
> wife, except for sexual immorality,
> makes her the victim of adultery,
> and anyone who marries a
> divorced woman commits adultery.
> **NIV**

This passage is sometimes misinterpreted to mean that sexual immorality means that a marriage must be terminated or that sexual immorality is an unpardonable offense against a spouse. The scriptures can be contextually used to refute this in the example given in Hosea 3:1-3:

> [1] The LORD said to me, "Go, show your love to your wife again, though she is loved by another man and is an adulteress. Love her as the LORD loves the Israelites, though they turn to other gods and love the sacred raisin cakes." [2] So I bought her for fifteen shekels of silver and about a homer and a lethek of barley. [3] Then I told her, "You are to live with me many days; you must not be a prostitute or be intimate with any man, and I will behave the same way toward you." **NIV**

In the context of these scriptures, although Hosea's wife was an adulteress, a prostitute, and loved by another man, God called upon Hosea to not only show his love for his wife, but also to go to another man's home, buy his wife back with his own money, and forgive her of her sins against him so that they might live united together in marriage. As you can see, not only was Hosea not obligated to divorce his wife, but God also specifically called on him to forgive her and go to exceptionally great lengths to reconcile their relationship.

Regardless of where you are at in your marriage, the oneness that God has called for you to live with your spouse is indivisible and not intended for negotiation. Few relationships are in a place where a spouse is actually paying money to buy their spouse back from the bed of another suitor. However, this may be exactly what an estranged spouse may need to do in order to show their love toward their spouse despite the difficulties that they may face in their relationship. Every situation is different and fraught with its own set of perils and troubles. This example is given to us in the Bible to demonstrate the difference between truly doing everything in your power to preserve the oneness of a marriage and simply doing what the popular culture of society is willing to accept as being enough or reasonable. In truth, we tend to wimp out and not go the distance to make the sacrifices God has laid out for us to make in order to build a rewarding and fulfilling marriage.

Hosea makes an impressive level of sacrifice in this Biblical account in order to salvage and recover his marriage. Each of us should sincerely ask ourselves if we would do as Hosea did when God called on him to make this sacrifice for his marriage. Would you be quick to open your checkbook when faced with this situation or would you be reserved and hesitate? If you are married, you should talk candidly with your spouse about this in advance before you are faced with this kind of situation.

We had experienced disconnectedness after having been married for five years. At that time in our marriage, my husband informed me that he was no longer "in love" with me and did not really know if he was "meant to be married". This obviously broke my heart. However, at the same time, I wanted God to know that I would do whatever was within my power to save my marriage. So I asked my husband why he was not in love with me and found out that my physical appearance was not to his liking. In order to change this I underwent weight loss surgery to help me become more physically appealing to my husband. I had to get my husband to agree to give me at least one year for me to become the wife he thought he wanted and for God to work on his heart. Through much prayer and a deepened trust in God, all went well for us and we survived this test of being one flesh.

Certainly, there is such a thing as righteous negotiation in which man may argue with God in order to alter the math that may be applied to a situation. Abraham argued with God over the destruction of Sodom and Gomorrah, pleading his case before God that perhaps if 50, 45, or even 40 righteous men were found that God would relent and not destroy those wicked cities. As the story goes on, we discover that Abraham was not able to find so many righteous men within the walls of these cities. However, negotiating what God means by one flesh is foolhardy and likely to come only to the ruin of those who partake in this negotiation.

God's definition of one flesh is absolute and unmistakable. Much of what we find in the Bible is intended to define in detail how a married couple is to behave as one flesh. It also gives us cautionary tales on what may become of our marriage if we neglect God's direction and fail to unite in the manner in which God has prescribed for us.

Despite these age old definitions and explanations, we have surprisingly few examples or demonstrations of what it truly means to be one flesh. Based upon the examples and definitions we see in the Bible, we know a married couple is no longer two, but one flesh. However, there are few who actually live as though they truly believe or realize that they are an extension of their spouse. There is power in this kind of unity and it should not be merely glossed over with a glib or cliché assertion. The expression of unity in a marriage is a pure and holy thing that starts with a clear understanding of what a marriage really is and how it is supposed to work and operate. This oneness is supposed to be unique and is to remain unaltered throughout the lives of the married couple.

In this book, you will find that there is a significant amount of scripture quoted in order to convey points and articulate expressions as only God could express them. It is our firm belief that, although we may be able to assemble clever words or poetry, there are no words so powerful as the ones deemed by God Himself. The focus and basis of this book is to assemble scripture to build a context and framework by which God has spoken on the topic of marriage and how a marriage should manifest itself as one flesh.

After you...I insist

You must put your spouse's desires ahead of your own in order to learn how to think as they do. A properly functioning marriage in many ways resembles a waltz. In order for the dancer that is following to know where the leader is going or what the leader is trying to do, the follower must allow for the leader to make the first move.

Upon many occasions, Jesus spoke of some very profound mysteries that are seldom fully understood even to this day. In Matthew 20:25-28, Jesus talks about what is required of anyone that would seek to be great in God's kingdom:

> [25]Jesus called them together and said, "You know that the rulers of the Gentiles lord it over them, and their high officials exercise authority over them. [26] Not so with you. Instead, whoever wants to become great among you must be your servant, [27] and whoever wants to be first must be your slave— [28] just as the Son of Man did not come to be served, but to serve, and to give his life as a ransom for many." **NIV**

This multifaceted proverb helps to give us some insight into what it takes to truly be fulfilled in life because it illuminates the futility of the pursuit of selfish objectives.

The greatest position achievable in life is the position of servant or slave.

Almost everyone has experienced the position of submitting to an authority that can not or will not apologize for any of his or her mistakes. This lordship behavior was very typical of rulers in Jesus' day and still occurs quite often in modern days. Understanding how to avoid this behavior needs to begin from an appreciation for how it feels when someone lords over you and how grateful you should feel for the fact that God does not lord His authority over you, despite His ability and right to do so.

Greatness is not measured in the possessions of man, nor the quantity or quality of the things he does. Rather, greatness is measured in the humility that is shown in the heart of a man or woman who would otherwise be revered beyond his or her peers. Greatness requires self-control and discipline to withstand the pressures of society that would encourage selfishness and self-indulgence.

Jesus has called His followers to put off the self-indulgences of the world and become great through personal sacrifice and servitude. In everything, we should think and act as though we are servants. Jesus gave us an example of how we should behave in Luke 17:7-10:

> [7] "Suppose one of you has a
> servant plowing or looking after
> the sheep. Will he say to the
> servant when he comes in from the
> field, 'Come along now and sit
> down to eat'? [8] Won't he rather
> say, 'Prepare my supper, get
> yourself ready and wait on me
> while I eat and drink; after that
> you may eat and drink'? [9] Will he
> thank the servant because he did
> what he was told to do? [10] So you
> also, when you have done
> everything you were told to do,
> should say, 'We are unworthy
> servants; we have only done our
> duty.'"   **NIV**

Having the attitude of a servant, we should serve having
neither desire nor expectation for appreciation or
recognition. In the end, if we do everything that God has
commanded for us to do in our marriage and life, then our
servant attitude should be that we are unworthy servants
that have merely done our duty.

When serving your spouse, it is vitally important
that your service comes not with an expectation for
appreciation, but with a desire to love and serve
regardless of how this service is met or acknowledged. A
servant that puts their master first is a servant that truly
understands what it means to be a mere servant. The

attitude with which you serve your spouse is equally as important as the actions of servitude you take.

As a Godly wife, the Proverbs 31 Wife of Noble Character does well to and for her husband because she knows this is pleasing to God. She is not considered noble because her husband is noble or treats her in a noble way, but rather because her husband's behavior is irrelevant to her duties as a wife. She is noble because of her wisdom, strength, and ability to serve with a happy heart for it is the Lord she fears. This kind of service is looked upon favorably by God.

Serving your spouse while grumbling or complaining about your service is a sure fire way to have this effort received poorly. If you are going to begrudgingly serve your spouse, then you may as well not try to serve your spouse at all. Before you presume to take on the position of your spouse's servant, check your heart and examine your motivation. Duty and obligation are not sincere factors that will be appreciated when serving your spouse. Your spouse deserves more than just your duty and obligation. Your spouse deserves for you to serve them with your whole heart, for no other reason than simply because you love them and want to please them.

Whenever my husband comes home, I know it pleases him when the house is nice and tidy. Therefore, a part of my every day includes tidying up the house and having our children put away their toys. Since my husband knows I try to please him and show my love in this way, he has the freedom to invite anyone at anytime to visit our home and can expect the home to be tidy and neat in appearance.

Why you serve your spouse is just as important as how you serve your spouse. In the course of life, there will no doubt be times when you serve your spouse out of duty. However, this cannot be the defining reason for why you serve your spouse. More often than not, you need to serve your spouse from the wellspring of your very own personal desire.

Serving your spouse means that you must take an accurate accounting of the things that actually please your spouse. Buying golf clubs for your spouse when they hate everything in the world about golf sends them a message that you do not care enough about them to know or pay attention to what they like or enjoy. Your service that you offer to your spouse must always be both timely and meaningful.

The sacrificial surrender of your entire identity is only a part of what is required to be a part of God's kingdom. Jesus explains the level of sacrifice he requires in Luke 14:25-28:

²⁵ Large crowds were traveling with Jesus, and turning to them he said: ²⁶ "If anyone comes to me and does not hate father and mother, wife and children, brothers and sisters—yes, even their own life—such a person cannot be my disciple. ²⁷ And whoever does not carry their cross and follow me cannot be my disciple. ²⁸ "Suppose one of you wants to build a tower. Won't you first sit down and estimate the cost to see if you have enough money to complete it? ²⁹ For if you lay the foundation and are not able to finish it, everyone who sees it will ridicule you, ³⁰ saying, 'This person began to build and wasn't able to finish.' ³¹ "Or suppose a king is about to go to war against another king. Won't he first sit down and consider whether he is able with ten thousand men to oppose the one coming against him with twenty thousand? ³²If he is not able, he will send a delegation while the other is still a long way off and will ask for terms of peace. ³³ In the same way, those of you who do not give up everything you have cannot be my disciples. **NIV**

Forfeiture of all sense of family and occupation is really just the beginning of what God expects from His followers. To hate your father and mother and even your own life is to take away all of the worldly ways of identifying yourself and relying solely on the Lord for your existence. On its own, this is a broad and impractical measure. So broad, that some scholars incorrectly question if this is truly what Jesus meant to say in this discourse. However, we can consider some thoughts to give us an idea of what it may have been meant to look like in our lives.

Often times, examining how to apply scripture to your life requires the unimpeded view of an objective third party perspective. To hate your father, mother, and life may mean one thing for one person and mean something significantly different to another. Learning to submit your will to the will of another requires not only discipline and self control, but also a desire to relinquish your own goals and objectives in order that someone else's objectives may be obtained. Hating your father and mother is directly related to the style and type of relationship that you have with your parents. For some people, parental relationships are heavily laden with a desire to please or prove worth. Hating your father and mother for these people would mean to surrender the desire to win the praise and admiration of your parents and place above it, the desire to win the praise and admiration of God. This does not mean that for this reason you should in any way disrespect your parents, but rather that you would deny the desires of your heart to please them in order to align your priorities to allow for you to please God first. Figuring out your own personal struggles with family and personal life priorities can best be done with the help of an outside person examining your life with an impartial eye.

This scripture in Luke is often difficult for us to tackle because it requires that we consider not only our motivation behind our relationships, but also how they may be perceived by others. After dashing our selfish motivations for maintaining familial relationships, Jesus proceeds to have us examine the outcomes of our behaviors and consider how others might perceive us. Empirically, one might assume that if you fail to count the cost of building a tower and leave a building in ruins that this is simply a problem for you and you alone. However, Jesus called on people to consider the example or legacy that is being left behind by the actions they choose to take. As Christians, we are always living examples of what God expects from mankind. Failing to live a righteous example confuses non-Christians and misrepresents God.

In the context of this scripture in Luke 14, Jesus is talking about the cost that must be paid in order for an individual to be counted as His disciple. People in Jesus' day understood quite well the humiliation that typically accompanies the rule of a foreign nation. Even though the Israelites actually fought (unsuccessfully) for the Romans in order to help them defeat the Parthians in Jewish battles fought between 40-37BC, it was not long before they did not appreciate or desire the requirements of life under Roman rule. Jews of this time understood the difference between being "subjects" of the Parthian empire and "clients" of the Roman Empire, the latter allowing for them to maintain their own king and relatively unimpeded rule of law. In modern days, fewer people in the world still see these oppressive lordship structures. Perhaps the world may never be totally free from this, but a great many people are able to enjoy life in a manner that can make it difficult to relate to what it means to surrender absolutely everything in order to please the master that rules over you. In the course of history, the Jewish temple treasury was robbed several times when wars were lost. Foreigners entered the holy place of the temple and took everything of value and kept it for themselves. Meanwhile, the Jewish people could only look on as their captors impressed their will upon them.

Learning to surrender everything in your life is the only way for you to be able to truly be submissive and follow your spouse. Jesus set a perfect example for us to follow in that He lived his life as a servant even though as the creator of the universe, He had every right to demand that all of His subjects serve Him. In John 13:3-8, Jesus explains this:

> ³ Jesus knew that the Father had put all things under his power, and that he had come from God and was returning to God; ⁴ so he got up from the meal, took off his outer clothing, and wrapped a towel around his waist. ⁵ After that, he poured water into a basin and began to wash his disciples' feet, drying them with the towel that was wrapped around him. ⁶ He came to Simon Peter, who said to him, "Lord, are you going to wash my feet?" ⁷ Jesus replied, "You do not realize now what I am doing, but later you will understand." ⁸ "No," said Peter, "you shall never wash my feet." Jesus answered, "Unless I wash you, you have no part with me." **NIV**

In order for us to put others first as Jesus did, we must shed our expectations of our own self-induced importance and take on the position of a servant.

Jesus' servant nature is often discussed in many Christian narratives and books. We suspect that this is at least in part because talking about it is much more easily done than actually putting it into practice. Practically speaking, we are the people who emerge when we are in the most difficult of situations. Companies sometimes intentionally try to place prospective employees into challenging or stressful situations during interview processes in order to gauge future behavior and determine relative strengths and weaknesses. In much the same way, the manner in which we live with our spouse is most often felt not by how we behave when we are involved in simple situations. On the contrary, our true nature is exposed when we are at our most vulnerable and the situation is at odds with our desires. Sometimes, your spouse may measure you entirely by how you react to difficult situations and completely ignore the fact that once you walk out of church on Sunday, you are the most spiritual person on the face of the earth. A servant does not plead his case for fair treatment because he recognizes his life is not his own.

In order to have a faithful part in a marriage, you must serve your spouse and allow for your spouse to serve you. Just as Jesus was not required to serve His disciples, you are not required to serve your spouse. However, in order for you to have a part in your relationship with your spouse, there must be a mutual edification of servitude one to another.

Shortly after we were married we both learned that serving each other was going to be difficult. Part of the reason for this was because we both wanted to please the other. Therefore, we both learned how to dismiss our wants and desires in order to allow the other's wants and desires to be met. It seems we keep trying to think of what the other's wants and desires might be, in order to serve them. This may sound like a vicious circle, but it is one that works for us and allows us to believe we are serving each other's needs by denying our own.

Putting your spouse first is a lifetime commitment and requires a passionate pursuit of patience and humility. Jesus set an example for us in service to those that might otherwise be held in lower regard than Himself. In doing this, Jesus had to suffer opposition from those that thought in everything, Jesus alone should be served. While this was rightly so, Jesus patiently taught His followers how to be followers and servants themselves. It does not matter if you are the head person in charge in your place of work. In your home, you must see to it that you are last in everything. Humility is the act of placing others ahead of yourself and recognizing that you yourself are full of faults. For it is written in Romans 3:21-26:

> **21** But now apart from the law the righteousness of God has been made known, to which the Law and the Prophets testify. **22** This righteousness is given through faith in Jesus Christ to all who

believe. There is no difference
between Jew and Gentile, [23] for all
have sinned and fall short of the
glory of God, [24] and all are
justified freely by his grace through
the redemption that came by Christ
Jesus. [25]God presented Christ as a
sacrifice of atonement, through the
shedding of his blood—to be
received by faith. He did this to
demonstrate his righteousness,
because in his forbearance he had
left the sins committed beforehand
unpunished — [26] he did it to
demonstrate his righteousness at
the present time, so as to be just
and the one who justifies those
who have faith in Jesus.   **NIV**

Keeping this in perspective, we should expect that on any
given day, we should find ourselves sincerely apologizing
to our spouse at least once because we sin against them
each day. You should note that if you find this difficult
because you do not have enough interaction with your
spouse, you should sincerely apologize for not investing
enough time in your spouse every day. A truly humble
person seeks to excel in recognizing when he or she has
sinned against others so that he or she can make amends,
learn, and grow in his or her righteousness.

Apologizing sincerely from the heart is very much undervalued in American society. Sincere apologies are very much appreciated, but it seems that few people have taken the time to learn to pursue this art. Surely, this is never taught properly in any of our schools. The pursuit of humility and apologies has never been a course taught at any school we have ever attended. However, to the contrary, we have never met a spouse that did not appreciate a sincere apology. As a framework to help guide us in the right direction let us take some time to look at what a truly sincere apology may look like.

A truly sincere apology should never come under duress. In the busyness of life I, at times, find that my schedule is somewhat in conflict with my wife's schedule. I have, at times, scheduled things on my calendar that prevented me from getting home in time for my wife to make a timely attendance to her schedule. A sincere apology is not one that occurs once my wife finds out that I scheduled carelessly. As soon as I realize my mistake, I need to aggressively seek out an opportunity to apologize and be the first to recognize my mistake. If I wait until my wife finds out I disrespected her schedule, then it is too late to make a sincere apology because at that point I am under duress and can only apologize because it is obvious that I have an obligation to do so.

A truly sincere apology comes from someone that wants to apologize and ensures that they do not repeat the same mistake in the future. Many parents begin to teach their children to apologize for misbehavior at very young ages. This is a good and cordial behavior. However, parents often fail to understand why this can so easily become ineffective and meaningless. When children apologize, they do so because they are told to do so and as such are obligated to apologize. In addition to being taught how to apologize, children must also be taught why they need to apologize, and still yet they must develop a heart of concern for others that provokes them to apologize. Concern for others can only be taught to a limited degree. Each individual must choose for them self whether or not they want to put others before them self. A framework and pattern can be set before an individual, but the choice to be humble or proud remains solely in the possession of the individual.

A truly sincere apology is a commitment to be different in the future. I once knew a man who apologized to his wife for cheating on her. While making his plea, he continued to live with his wife despite the fact that he continued to cheat on her with his mistress. Strangely enough, this may even be a story of common occurrence. It makes one contemplate and question the motivation behind the apology. Was he sorry because his wife found out what he was doing? Was he sorry because he hurt his wife's feelings? Was he concerned at all about whether or not his actions were right or wrong? In 2 Corinthians 7:8-11, Paul talks about the attitude we should have when we apologize:

> **8** Even if I caused you sorrow by my letter, I do not regret it. Though I did regret it—I see that my letter hurt you, but only for a little while— **9** yet now I am happy, not because you were made sorry, but because your sorrow led you to repentance. For you became sorrowful as God intended and so were not harmed in any way by us. **10** Godly sorrow brings repentance that leads to salvation and leaves no regret, but worldly sorrow brings death. **11** See what this godly sorrow has produced in you: what earnestness, what eagerness to clear yourselves, what indignation, what alarm, what longing, what concern, what readiness to see justice done. At every point you have proved yourselves to be innocent in this matter.   **NIV**

Repentance always follows a truly sincere apology. In this scripture, Paul is talking about how the purpose behind worldly sorrow is "to get away with wrongdoing" and how it differs from Godly sorrow. Godly sorrow is followed by a change of heart and mind that produces different future results on account of a passionate desire to be right with God. This passage draws an illustration of eager attempts to clear oneself of wrongdoing and readiness to see justice done. Since we know that we all make mistakes, we must all eagerly seek to correct those wrongs and not wait until we are no longer given a choice to do what is right.

Early in our marriage, I used anger as a weapon against my husband to feel heard. I knew that being quick to anger was not Godly and I knew it was not effective in establishing my voice in the marriage. After a patient and slow to anger husband pointed out my constant angry moods, we both agreed that I would seek some much needed anger counseling. Even though the counseling went well and I learned how to control my anger, it was really my deep desire to be pleasing to God and have the kind of marriage He so desired for me that empowered me to be a different woman. To this day, neither my husband nor I can remember the last time we had a true argument. That is not to say we never disagree, but that we are both very slow to anger, discuss and communicate how we feel rather than trying to use tactics to beat the other into submission.

In Paul's case, the recognition that something has gone wrong often causes an amount of friction or adversity within a relationship. Even Paul acknowledges that for a time, he regretted the fact that he had to point out that the church in Corinth was in need of changing its ways. Likewise, when we see the need to point out sin in our spouse's lives, this will often hurt our spouse initially, but if they change on account of our admonition; our relationship will be healed so that there was never any harm done to one another.

Respecting the needs of your spouse can not only be done when it is easy or convenient for you to do so. At times, putting your spouse first will mean that you must let them know when there is a serious sinful attitude in their heart that needs to change. This is seldom an easy conversation to have with your spouse. God has paired the two of you together so that you will form a union that is stronger than a sole individual.

When we recognize that we have made a mistake, we need to have the eager alarm that the Corinthians had when addressing our errors. The church in Corinth spared no effort in seeing to it that their church was not a place that tolerated sin in its midst. By actively engaging and addressing the sin in the congregation, the church in Corinth was able to prove themselves innocent in the matter because they saw to it the sin was followed by repentance.

In Luke 19:1-8, we see the story of Zacchaeus:

> [1] Jesus entered Jericho and was passing through. [2] A man was there by the name of Zacchaeus; he was a chief tax collector and was wealthy. [3] He wanted to see who Jesus was, but because he was short he could not see over the crowd. [4] So he ran ahead and climbed a sycamore-fig tree to see him, since Jesus was coming that way. [5] When Jesus reached the spot, he looked up and said to him, "Zacchaeus, come down immediately. I must stay at your house today." [6] So he came down at once and welcomed him gladly. [7] All the people saw this and began to mutter, "He has gone to be the guest of a sinner." [8] But Zacchaeus stood up and said to the Lord, "Look, Lord! Here and now I give half of my possessions to the poor, and if I have cheated anybody out of anything, I will pay back four times the amount." **NIV**

The story of Zacchaeus gives us an example of how we should apologize to someone when we have wronged them. If it is within our power, we should not only make restitution, but we should also pay back four times the amount that we owe them. This example is given to us to help us understand the difference between simply doing what is reasonably required of us and earnestly doing the very best that we can to serve others.

If Zacchaeus had cheated someone, then obviously he owed them their money back at a minimum. Paying them back four times the amount he had cheated them was intended to make amends for mistakes he may have made out of carelessness, but sincerely wanted to correct without causing harm to anyone. The excessive payback in this case was the means by which he could offer a truly sincere apology. This apology was intended to send a clear message that he was sorry for his mistake and that continuing to make this mistake would personally hurt him significantly as he continued to pay people back four times the amount of his errors.

The Zacchaeus story is a great example of a practical tool that we can use in everyday life to help us ensure that we are truly sorry when we apologize. While the specifics will vary for each and every individual couple, consider this scenario: Husband comes home late from work without calling or giving any kind of advanced notice and misses dinner with the family. Husband then has to make personal time for each person in the family by cancelling personal activities that the husband would otherwise do for himself. In addition to spending personal time with each family member, he must also make up the time that he missed when he should have spent time with the family all together. In this scenario, the husband is indebted to the family and owes them his time and attention. The willingness to sacrifice something personal of his own in order to make amends for his mistake helps him to ensure that he will not continue to make this mistake in the future. Much like in the story of Zacchaeus, the time restored should be four times the amount of time that was lost.

We need to set such an example in our humility that our spouse has no choice but to recognize we are worthy of both their respect and admiration. Some practical questions you should ask yourself are "Who is usually the first person in your marriage to apologize?" and "Who in your marriage apologizes the most?" Once you honestly answer these questions for yourself and recognize who is setting the lead example of humility in your marriage, you have to make a decision on which you are really going to be. If your spouse is leading the way in humility, do not accept that as the way things have to be. Immediately see to it that you outdo them by aggressively seeking opportunities to own your responsibility in every situation no matter how small it may seem to you initially. If you are already leading the way in your readiness to accept responsibility for your errors and mistakes, then honestly ask yourself if you are doing everything you can do to apologize in every situation in which you have done wrong. If Jesus would have been more humble had he been in any of your life situations, then you should strive to do likewise.

True humility will not occur in your life by happenstance. You must make a decision every day that you love God so much that you are willing to sacrifice your ego and live your life in such a way that you set an example of humility for everyone in the world. In order to learn to be humble, you must start by insisting that your spouse be honored above you in everything and that you always believe the best in all of your spouse's intentions. Real humility is tenacious and unwilling to accept anything other than the very best possible effort to apologize and be different, even after committing even the slightest of offenses.

Jesus laid out for us the ultimate example of humility in the way He lived among us on this earth. Paul summarizes this humility in Philippians 2:5-11:

> **5** In your relationships with one another, have the same mindset as Christ Jesus: **6** Who, being in very nature God, did not consider equality with God something to be

used to his own advantage;
7 rather, he made himself nothing
by taking the very nature of a
servant, being made in human
likeness. **8** And being found in
appearance as a man, he humbled
himself by becoming obedient to
death— even death on a cross!
9 Therefore God exalted him to the
highest place and gave him the
name that is above every name,
10 that at the name of Jesus every
knee should bow, in heaven and on
earth and under the earth, **11** and
every tongue acknowledge that
Jesus Christ is Lord, to the glory of
God the Father.   **NIV**

For those of us that may think we have reason to boast or
deserve to be honored or recognized for who we are or
what we have done, Jesus surpasses us all. However, even
though in His very nature, He is God, He did not use this as
leverage to exalt Himself above others. Likewise, we as
mere mortals should not exalt ourselves above others and
least of all not exalt ourselves above our spouse in
anything. In comparison to the qualifications of Jesus, the
things that we use to exalt ourselves here on earth are
comical and obviously meaningless.

If the creator of the universe made Himself nothing
and became the servant of all His created things, how

much more should we serve others and especially our spouse with whom we share our lives? This pattern is given to us as a faithful example of how God wants to work in and through our lives. Through Jesus' humility, a sacrifice was able to be made on this earth and after that sacrifice; God exalted Him to the highest place. God's exaltation cannot come to any of us without sacrifice, obedience, and humility. Just as all of these elements were required even of Jesus, so they are required of us.

In your marriage, you need to set an example of servitude. Just as Jesus served us in His life on earth, we should serve each other starting first with serving our spouse. A good daily goal should be to lighten the load of your spouse. See to it that in everything, you are taking on the nature of Jesus in serving your spouse. Exert effort in your servitude so that when your spouse has ended his or her day and as much as it depends upon you, his or her life will be easy upon them. Do this knowing that in time, God will exalt you for your sacrifice and obedience to His word.

If you should find that in your marriage your spouse is bearing more of the relationship's load than you are, do not accept this. If you should at all find a place in your relationship in which you should be competitive with one another, compete so that you can serve your spouse more than your spouse serves you. Make frequent assessments of this situation and see to it that in

One flesh

everything you are working as hard as you can to serve your spouse and make their life a joy.

Communication is key

Over time, I have been convinced through observation that I communicate with my spouse more than any other married couple I know. Communication in the body of a marriage begins with the example of biblical leadership and within any other body. Some part of the body must be the head. There needs to be a central place for leadership so that the body can function properly.

A common misconception about Christianity is that the scriptures somehow espouse throwback misogynistic values of a bygone era. This is most certainly not the case, but could potentially be construed if scripture is not examined carefully. In order for a body to function, the head must instruct the other members of the body to operate. This role however does not in any way diminish the importance of the other members of the body. When we closely examine the role of the body later on, it becomes quite evident that the role of the head is clearly not paramount.

The order in a marriage is defined in Ephesians 5:21-33:

> [21] Submit to one another out of reverence for Christ. [22] Wives, submit yourselves to your own husbands as you do to the Lord. [23] For the husband is the head of the wife as Christ is the head of the church, his body, of which he is the

Savior. **²⁴**Now as the church submits to Christ, so also wives should submit to their husbands in everything. **²⁵** Husbands, love your wives, just as Christ loved the church and gave himself up for her **²⁶** to make her holy, cleansing her by the washing with water through the word, **²⁷** and to present her to himself as a radiant church, without stain or wrinkle or any other blemish, but holy and blameless. **²⁸** In this same way, husbands ought to love their wives as their own bodies. He who loves his wife loves himself. **²⁹** After all, no one ever hated their own body, but they feed and care for their body, just as Christ does the church — **³⁰** for we are members of his body. **³¹** "For this reason a man will leave his father and mother and be united to his wife, and the two will become one flesh." **³²** This is a profound mystery—but I am talking about Christ and the church. **³³** However, each one of you also must love his wife as he loves himself, and the wife must respect her husband.   **NIV**

Marriages fail to function as one when the head does not communicate with the other parts of the body. This scripture articulates many aspects of how the marriage is to function. As the head of the body, it is vitally important that the husband communicates prolifically in support of the bodily functions and operation. Some scholars believe that men are not good communicators. This cannot be in the body of a marriage. Failure to communicate will starve the body of nutrients and development.

Although men are not well known for having good communication skills, this does not mean that they cannot learn how to communicate in a way that makes their marriage function properly. From the beginning of our marriage, it was easy to see I had the gift of communication. However, as an educator, I had to learn how to teach my husband how to communicate in a manner that allowed our marriage to thrive. Even though we still communicate in our own styles, the fact that any communication happens far exceeds the displays of communication we see in the marriages that surround us. Regardless of how the communication happens, the key is for both the husband and wife to communicate their day, their lives, and their needs with one another to allow for the two to truly become one.

The leadership of a man in a marriage extends farther than just communication and is neither misogynistic nor dated. The order is established to achieve a clear purpose. The first and most obvious point is that there has to be a leader in the marriage. If both the husband and the wife are the head, then how will either know in which direction he or she is to go? If the husband and wife have children, how will the children know from which of the parents to take direction? Two heads empowers the child to play one head against the other and choose to follow the head of greater convenience in any given situation.

The head must at all times be aware of the comings and goings of all parts of the body. As the leader of the marriage, the husband must be accountable to his wife, discussing in great detail the thoughts and dealings of every day's activities. This is done out of love. This is part of how a husband is to feed and care for the parts of his body. The singular mind of a truly one flesh marriage communicates and receives feedback from the body so that it can understand what the body needs and how to help it to grow and flourish.

When a wife submits to her husband, she takes great risk. She places her fate into the hands of a mortal, sinful man and trusts that God alone will sustain her. This submission is to extend even as far as obedience. Abraham's wife, Sarah, submitted herself completely and in Genesis 18:12, she called Abraham her lord. This is elaborated upon in 1 Peter 3:1-7:

[1] Wives, in the same way submit yourselves to your own husbands so that, if any of them do not believe the word, they may be won over without words by the behavior of their wives, [2] when they see the purity and reverence of your lives. [3] Your beauty should not come from outward adornment, such as elaborate hairstyles and the wearing of gold jewelry or fine clothes. [4] Rather, it should be that of your inner self, the unfading beauty of a gentle and quiet spirit, which is of great worth in God's sight. [5] For this is the way the holy women of the past who put their hope in God used to adorn themselves. They submitted themselves to their own husbands, [6] like Sarah, who obeyed Abraham and called him her lord. You are her daughters if you do what is right and do not give way to fear.

[7] Husbands, in the same way be considerate as you live with your wives, and treat them with respect as the weaker partner and as heirs with you of the gracious gift of life, so that nothing will hinder your prayers. **NIV**

This kind of submission has been obvious in our marriage any time we have moved our family from one state to another. Whenever my husband has indicated a desire to move, I have done my best to submit to his desires and plans for our family's future. I have to put my trust in him and have faith that God will provide for our needs, regardless of whether or not the decision was a good one. This level of submission allows for my husband to lead and gives him the support that he needs to make the decisions he feels are guided by God. Any manner of interference does not allow for my husband to be submitted to God, as I submit to him.

Sarah set a Godly example of submission in her recognition of her husband as her lord. In this submissive state, she placed her trust not in her husband's lordship, but rather in the Lord that was leading him. Like Sarah, wives are called upon by God to submit themselves to their husbands and follow the direction in which they are being led.

Communication is intimately tied to the manner in which a husband is to be considerate of his wife. The wife cannot give way to fear when submitting to her husband. The husband cannot be considerate of his wife if he is not in touch with the desires, cares, and passions of his wife. Communication is clearly being defined in the above scripture as both what a husband says and how he listens to his wife. Furthermore, in failing to be considerate of his wife, this scripture promises that the husband's prayers will be hindered. It must be impressed upon the husband the seriousness of not listening to his wife and being considerate of her.

In this same manner, my husband has always asked me my desires when questioning whether or not to move our family. He has learned to listen to my thoughts regarding the decision and figures out a way to meet them, even if they do not align with his thoughts. By voicing my desires and allowing for my husband to go to God in prayer we give God the opportunity to answer our prayers and meet both of our needs, regardless of the outcome. However, if we had not taken the time to communicate and listen to each other we would not have been considerate of each other's feelings regarding the moves and any and all of our prayers would have been hindered.

Imagine the visual image presented in this case: when someone is lord over you, they have the ultimate power over you. They have the authority to decide whether you live or die, eat or starve, take shelter, or freeze. Lordship is not something to take lightly. Submitting to someone as if they are your lord means that you surrender absolutely all of your authority over your own body and existence to someone or something else.

You retain no rights to keep for yourself. As your lord prospers you, so do you prosper. As your lord withholds from you, you go in want. In this lordship relationship, you have no right to raise a complaint of any kind.

All too often, we feel as though we deserve to be treated in certain ways. However in reality, we do not actually deserve anything. Submission is only possible through humility. Humility is the recognition that you are not the creator of your own life. You were not created for the purpose of serving yourself, but rather for the purpose of serving God. As God's servant on earth, you are no better than any of your fellow humankind. For a wife, submission to God's will necessarily means submission to her husband in everything. This choice is for her to make and she must seriously consider the risk and weigh the benefits and rewards that may lie ahead of her.

Submission to mortal men is often foolhardy when men are ungodly, but this is never the case with Godly men. This should not be confused to mean that following Godly men will lead to fame and fortune, but rather that the outcome of your life will lead to the development of Godly character. This Godly character could lead to fame and fortune, though not necessarily. An ungodly man may pray to God and yet have his prayers unheard or hindered. A man who does not listen to his wife has a broken relationship with God in that although he may cry out to

God, his prayers may be hindered. God allows for this break in His relationship to occur in order to persuade men to listen to their wives. This prayer hindrance is an opportunity for the husband to see his need for God and for God to ensure that the wife is not neglected.

Ungodly men are often too preoccupied with themselves to immediately notice that God is not with them in their lives. Their lives are just as miserable before they ignored their wives as it was when they listened to their wives. The dynamic flow in their lives is not noticeable to them because of other sin in their lives that also hinders their prayers as described in Isaiah 59:1-2:

> [1] Surely the arm of the LORD is not too short to save, nor his ear too dull to hear. [2] But your iniquities have separated you from your God; your sins have hidden his face from you, so that he will not hear.　　**NIV**

When God will not listen to your prayers, this is a terrifying situation. Your success or failure in life is almost entirely up to you at that point and your eternity is doomed no matter what worldly accolades you may manage to achieve.

Communication is as much about what is being said as it is about how it is being said. Let us consider Ephesians 4:29:

> **29** Do not let any unwholesome talk come out of your mouths, but only what is helpful for building others up according to their needs, that it may benefit those who listen.
>
> **NIV**

Unwholesome talk can manifest itself as an attitude, tone, or simply gossip. Many relationships that are supposed to be Godly actually have some very bad communication patterns. In the workplace, we often treat our coworkers with a degree of courtesy and respect. We avoid talking down to people or using a derogatory tone out of concern for our fellow worker. Oddly enough our spouses, for whom we say we have the most concern, do not always get this same level of respect from us. This really should not be the way we interact with our loved ones. The people we love should get our very best level of concern and respect from us. This means that it is never appropriate for us to raise our voices at them. It is never appropriate for us to marginalize them. It is never appropriate for us to ignore their ideas, beliefs, or concerns. In everything, we must strive to build each other up. Speaking to one another without regard for the tone of our conversation does not place the hearer in a position where they can easily benefit from the message that is being spoken. Effective communication always strives to put the hearer in the best possible position. When communicating with your spouse, always put forth your best effort to speak carefully and slowly. The objective here is to ensure that there is actually someone listening on the other end of the communication.

One way of ensuring that someone is actually listening is making sure that person is not in the middle of something else. It did not take me very long in our marriage to realize that when my husband was watching sports on television or working on his computer that this was not a good time to have a serious conversation with him. I had to learn to read when he was not busy or just ask if we could talk. My husband also had to learn that when I asked if he was busy or could talk, there was something weighing heavy on my heart that I needed to talk about. In other words, we both learned that to communicate effectively meant we both had to be ready to listen.

Often times, your spouse may want for you to respond to something when you are not in a position to respond in a Godly manner. Sometimes anger can be a barrier that prevents an individual from faithfully communicating in a manner that is helpful for building up others. This is a case when you should refrain from speaking. If you cannot live out this command from God, then you need to get your heart into a place where you will be able to do so. Once you have been able to resolve your anger and move past the reason why you could not build up your spouse with your speech, then you should respond in a manner that benefits those who listen.

Communication is not just something you are supposed to do. Communication needs to have a clear purpose. Much in the same way that you would converse with a non-Christian, your conversation should have realistic expectations of growth in the faith. In Colossians 4:6, we read:

> **⁶** Let your conversation be always full of grace, seasoned with salt, so that you may know how to answer everyone.   **NIV**

Likewise, with your spouse, your conversation should always be full of grace. When conversing, it is of paramount importance that you are listening intently so that you may know how to appropriately answer all with whom you may be communicating.

Communication is something that requires a lot of effort to do effectively. Some people struggle with communication throughout their lives. Each person is equipped with his or her own capacity for communication and while this capacity may grow over time, it may yet have limits. Wherever you and your spouse may be at in your capacities for communication, you need to supply sufficient grace to allow for each member of the marriage to be heard and understood.

In everything you must believe the best in your spouse when they are trying to communicate with you. If it is possible to interpret that they are trying to insult you and likewise interpret that they are trying to understand you, choose the understanding that is more favorable for your spouse and assume that they are merely trying to understand you. Grace in communication is absolutely necessary as each person works out his or her skill in expressing him or herself.

Communication needs to be something you enjoy. Good communication stems from a relationship in which both parties are eagerly intent on communicating with each other. A righteous person wants not only to have influence in the life of his or her spouse, but also wants to hear what is going on in their lives and take an active role in the activity of their spouse. This can only happen through effective, positive communication. This sort of communication feeds on itself. A truly loving relationship breeds the desire to communicate. When you care about someone else, you not only want to share your life with them, but you also eagerly want for them to share their life with you. Paul talks about this in 1 Thessalonians 2:6-8:

> **6** We were not looking for praise from people, not from you or anyone else, even though as apostles of Christ we could have asserted our authority. **7** Instead, we were like young children among you. Just as a nursing mother cares for her children, **8** so we cared for you. Because we loved you so much, we were delighted to share with you not only the gospel of God but our lives as well.
>
> **NIV**

Selfless, loving communication does not seek praise. Probably everyone knows, or at one time has known, someone that likes to parade about the coming and goings of their life in order to receive praise from other people. This is not what communication is about. This type of communication leads to an unhealthy view of yourself. This is warned against in Romans 12:3:

> **3** For by the grace given me I say to every one of you: Do not think of yourself more highly than you ought, but rather think of yourself with sober judgment, in accordance with the faith God has

distributed to each of you.

NIV

This kind of self exultation prevents you from examining yourself with sober judgment. Without sober judgment, it is impossible to recognize when your communication is offensive.

Some of the most unproductive, unspiritual communication within marriages is offensive or malicious talk. Pop culture would have you believe that men are supposed to be insensitive and unaware of their offensive behavior. This is not the case. This perspective is nothing more than an excuse for laziness. If a man expends the effort to learn how not to be offensive in his speech, he more than likely can learn how to avoid this. It is absolutely possible to teach old dog new tricks, despite what you may have heard in old wives' tales. Avoiding offensive talk requires sober judgment and concern for the manner with which you speak.

The discussions, or should I say arguments, that happened early in our marriage were riddled with offensive talk on my part. My husband would always try to refrain from any offensive talk or behavior, even if I had argued him into a corner. Through the benefits of anger counseling and my walk with God, I learned how to control my tongue and use loving words to express how I felt without belittling my husband. That step was not easy to conquer, as I felt my self-esteem was always on the line when my husband and I were at odds. It was my faith and trust in God I had to rely on in order to change my reaction in such situations and to improve my relationship with my husband.

Jesus exhorted his disciples to live their lives like little children. In response, Paul spoke of his time with the Thessalonians as being like a child among them. Taking the example found in Matthew 18:2-5:

> [2] He called a little child to him, and placed the child among them. [3]And he said: "Truly I tell you, unless you change and become like little children, you will never enter the kingdom of heaven. [4]Therefore, whoever takes the lowly position of this child is the greatest in the kingdom of heaven. [5] And whoever welcomes one such child in my name welcomes me.
>
> **NIV**

Effective communication does not come from a position of power or arrogance. Effective communication comes from the realization that you are no more powerful than a little child. Effective communication stems from an appropriate view of God's authority over all mankind.

One flesh

On a daily basis, I find myself talking with my wife, recounting the day's activities. Typically, this is a very thorough and detailed conversation that takes at least a couple of hours. I have seen that as our relationship has evolved, we talk about more and more things that previously seemed trivial to me. As we have drawn closer and closer to one another, it has become quite apparent that we have developed a yearning for our relationship with each other. We have found ourselves not communicating solely for the purpose of operating the machinery of our marriage, picking up the kids and coordinating responsibilities, but we have found ourselves intently sharing our lives with one another as well.

Obviously, communication will be necessary so that a couple can understand who has a given responsibility. However, if this is the sole source of communication within a marriage, then the marriage is effectively dead. If your marriage is to be fruitful and provide fulfillment for both individuals, it has to have communication that entices each other to participate. If communication with your spouse is a dreary act of willful self-denial, it is highly unlikely that your communication will be effective or even consistent.

Human nature is such that we instinctively excel at the things we enjoy because these are the areas in our lives from which we receive the most enjoyment. Building a fun and functional pattern of communication starts with respecting and valuing one another. The husband must respect and value the wife, as the wife must respect and value the husband. This means that in your communication there can be no attitudes, raising of voices, or derogatory statements. Marital communication must be the only place where both members feel free to talk about absolutely anything and everything. Nothing should be taboo. Conversations about sexual pleasures, likes, and dislikes must certainly be discussed in the most candid of ways. Over time, there needs to be some review of how the relationship is going. Once a couple is married, ambitions, goals and dreams can and often do change over time. It is important to keep abreast of these changes so encouragement and uplifting can be timely and relevant.

Husbands often feel nagged when their spouses do not make requests of them in respectful ways. Often, the message given to the husband was less the issue than the manner in which it was delivered to them. Sometimes a better lead in to a request that has been made multiple times is to start off with a relevant apology relating to the specific situation. Sarcasm has no place in this conversation. Unwittingly, sarcasm often has unintended consequences for which the relationship will eventually have to pay.

One flesh

In the early years of our marriage, we found that our communication bore a greater resemblance to shouting matches than healthy conversation. During this time, we struggled to find a way to communicate with one another effectively without further exacerbating our situations. Often times, I would go silent during arguments and simply listen to what was being said without responding or giving any kind of feedback. Typically, I would barely acknowledge that I even heard what was being said. At one point, my wife suggested that if she could just hit me every time I said or did something that made her angry she would be happy. So I went to a local store and bought a swimming noodle and told her that she could hit me with the noodle as much as she wanted when she was angry, but if she did so, she was not permitted to yell or raise her voice at me when expressing her displeasure with whatever may have been bothering her. This method of beating to vent frustration and calm tone of discussion went on for about six months before we both learned to communicate effectively without the beatings.

In our case, beatings with a swimming noodle were a necessary tool in order for us to learn to communicate with each other effectively. For some people, this technique may result in spousal abuse, hospitalizations, and maybe even incarceration. Although we often share this example of broad-minded techniques, we certainly do not recommend it for everyone that we counsel on spousal communication. Every situation is different and every member in a marriage has a level of tolerance and willingness or capacity to grow. Learning to communicate with your spouse effectively begins with taking an honest assessment of your current bag of talents. If your bag is a golf bag and you have a driver, but don't know how to use it effectively, it is perfectly fine to pull out an iron and hit the ball confidently and effectively. It is important to remember that life is a game where keeping the ball on the fairway is more important than making par because ultimately, no one is keeping score. If you are able to get the ball in the hole without losing it, hurting a spectator, or falling out of bounds, then it is effectively the same thing as a hole in one.

Communication requires a commitment of time. In order to effectively communicate with your spouse, you must devote a significant amount of your time to them. One of the most common problems in marriages we have seen is a spouse who wants to live the life of a single person with a spouse on the side. More specifically, men often find themselves hanging out with "the guys" and enjoying themselves, while their pregnant wives are at home watching their children. This immature and insensitive behavior breeds dysfunctional communication. Invariably, these are the same men who find it difficult to have healthy communication with their spouses because they have not yet learned to place an appropriate value on this communication.

When I was a young and newly married man, I had not experienced any particular training on what married life would be like. I quickly found myself wondering if I should always feel the pressure of being around and available to my wife all of the time. I felt as if I was being smothered in some way because I did not have any opportunities to be by myself. I sought advice from a coworker of mine whom I knew to be a regular churchgoer, but not even remotely close to being the most Bible thumping guy I knew. I asked him if it was normal for a married man to be with their spouse on any and every occasion and not have any personal time to themselves. Without hesitating, he told me that there is nothing in this world that he would rather do than spend time with his wife and children. It was at this point that I realized I was the problem with spending time with my wife and needed to change my attitude. It was at this time that my view of my role in my marriage was forever altered. It became very clear and obvious to me that for me to be married, I had to make a commitment to my wife and love every single moment of time that I could spend with her. To love my wife is to seek out every opportunity I can spend with her and treasure it.

In this modern day, time is the currency of greatest value. Every one of us has a limited and finite amount of time on this earth as well as limited time in a given day. How we spend this time communicates a message to our spouse on where our values and priorities lie. Jesus expressed this concept best in Matthew 6:19-21:

> [19] "Do not store up for yourselves treasures on earth, where moths and vermin destroy, and where thieves break in and steal. [20] But store up for yourselves treasures in heaven, where moths and vermin do not destroy, and where thieves do not break in and steal. [21] For where your treasure is, there your heart will be also.   **NIV**

There will never be a shortage of things on which we can spend our time in futility. As we mature in our marriage, we learn that time spent away from our spouse is not only wasted or lost time, but it is also time that diminishes the value we place on our marriage in our own hearts.

The more time you spend convincing yourself that you do not need to be with your spouse, the more you will begin to believe this. This behavior is unhealthy communication of the worst kind because it not only sends a message to the person behaving in this manner, but it also communicates to the spouse that time spent with him or her is not valuable to you. The failure to invest your time in your spouse constantly erodes your marriage if you allow this behavior to persist.

On the contrary, good communication requires that quality time be spent with your spouse on a consistent basis. Your spouse needs for you to spend time with them because this time you spend communicates a value that you place on them and on your relationship. Newlywed couples often struggle to understand this because up until they have reached this point in their lives, there has been no reason for them to learn how to unite themselves with another person as one flesh and the examples that they have are almost always very poor.

Communicating the value that you place on your relationship with your spouse requires more than just your physical attendance in the home. Being present and not engaged communicates that you feel obligated to the relationship, but do not really value the relationship. This behavior undermines your spouse's self esteem because it is yet another way for you to tell your spouse that you really do not value them at all.

Good time communication requires engaging conversation. In order to be counted present in the company of your spouse, you must listen attentively, make good eye contact, and respond appropriately and respectfully. This time cannot be spent while you are engaged in other activities that could be confused with activities you enjoy over and above spending time with your spouse. This time needs to be time that you consciously dedicate to your spouse so that you can be involved in their life, encourage them, and help them if they need your assistance.

Spending time with your spouse should not be a passive activity. When your communication begins to develop some health, you should find that you engage in probing conversation to better and more fully understand one another. Active, engaging communication expresses a positive value that is placed on the relationship by those that are involved in this process.

If you do not treasure your spouse currently, but want to treasure your spouse, investing your time and heart will move you closer to your spouse than you are today. Even if you feel like you are close to your spouse, you can always get even closer by continuing to have engaging conversations. Over time, thoughts and feelings change and these changes can threaten to create a gap in your relationship. Staying close to your spouse requires constant, heartfelt and meaningful time spent in communication. With good communication your marriage can grow in a positive direction and become more of what God desired for marriage.

One flesh

One doctrine

One flesh

Some of the most interesting behavior that can be observed in today's "Christian" world is the belief that it is perfectly fine for one spouse to have one belief (or set of beliefs) and the other spouse to have radically different beliefs. Even some highly prominent church leaders have been known to have spouses that never attend the churches where they preach because they espouse different liturgical views. This leads one to the question "Can I have religious views that are different from the religious views of my spouse?" The answer to this question quite obviously is that of course you can have religious views that are different from your spouse, but not without consequence.

When a couple is one flesh, they live, breathe, think, and act out of a singular state of mind and beliefs. Human anatomy teaches us that the human brain consists of two prominent halves. These halves have different, yet important functions. Imagine if you will that one half of the brain believes that Jesus is the Messiah, the savior of the world, and the other half believes that the Messiah has not yet come, and God has not yet brought salvation to His people. While this is perhaps a more radical example than what is found in many marriages, the clinical term for this split-brained (theological) state is paranoid schizophrenia. God has been generous enough to allow for us to have the free will to choose to either follow His plan or not to follow His plan.

It is vitally important that you study the Bible with your spouse and agree on its interpretation because this will greatly influence the way you live your life. It would not be right if the wife expects for her husband to have seven wives and the husband believes that he can only have one. Studying the Bible together helps build a unifying doctrine of belief that empowers the couple to function as a single, unified flesh. Your belief structure is the foundation upon which your relationship will be built, so this must be managed extremely carefully.

As life events come and go, external events can sometimes alter or shift some foundational beliefs that a couple may have established. In order to keep in step with your spouse, you must periodically review your beliefs and doctrine to ensure that neither of you has strayed from the other in your commitment to God. With God being the unifying factor in your relationship, nothing can break your relationship. In Ecclesiastes 4:9-12 we find:

> [9] Two are better than one, because they have a good return for their labor: [10] If either of them falls down, one can help the other up. But pity anyone who falls and has no one to help them up. [11] Also, if two lie down together, they will keep warm. But how can one keep warm alone? [12] Though one may be overpowered, two can defend

themselves. A cord of three
strands is not quickly broken.

NIV

There are some important points that we can glean from this scripture. The context tells us that it is talking about marriage as the two are likely to lie down together. A cord of three strands implicitly tells us that the unifying factor between the two must be God and that the two alone would not be strong enough to endure every situation. Furthermore, if the two are not tied together in their relationship with God, then they would not be a cord of three strands and would therefore be subject to fragility.

Keeping God at the center of your relationship is a vital part of God's plan for every marriage on earth. Firmly establishing this relationship with God is much more easily said than done. Obviously, priorities play a significant role in our decisions on whether or not to study the Bible with our spouses, but sometimes genuine fear may be a factor. Feelings of inadequacy often serve as a distraction that can dissuade us from acting on righteous impulses that we know we should obey. In many ways, life is a complex balancing act that requires we keep the correct proportions of the right influences that we need in our lives.

Some of the most practical advice that I have used in my marriage has been to read through the Bible with your spouse, one chapter at a time. If you read together every day, it will take you three years to complete this task. In three year's time, you will have been married longer than the average length of a Unites States marriage. This daily Bible study is a great mechanism with which you can build a firm foundation for your faith together.

Unity of doctrine is such an essential Christian tenet, that Jesus Himself prayed about this oneness on the night before he was crucified. In John 17:20-23 Jesus prayed:

> [20] "My prayer is not for them alone. I pray also for those who will believe in me through their message, [21] that all of them may be one, Father, just as you are in me and I am in you. May they also be in us so that the world may believe that you have sent me. [22] I have given them the glory that you gave me, that they may be one as we are one— [23] I in them and you in me—so that they may be brought to complete unity. Then the world will know that you sent me and have loved them even as you have loved me. **NIV**

The love of Jesus' followers is represented in the unity that they share with one another. Just as Jesus and the Father are one, so should be all of His believers. This is especially true in a marriage because when the unity of doctrine is missing, it is felt more readily and directly by the spouse than it may be in other parts of the church.

If Jesus prayed this prayer for unity amongst his disciples, how much more should a married couple be united in their doctrine? In this passage, Jesus is expressing His desire that all of his followers be completely united. Clearly, it is not possible to be completely united if you lack unity in your most basic and fundamental doctrinal beliefs.

Complete unity means that you are united in every possible way. The complete unity that Jesus talks about here does not leave room for the possibility that there can be dissention in the body of believers. This can only be achieved through united Bible study and prayer.

In the church family as in the marital family, Jesus' prayer here is that there would be complete unity. Human laziness often precludes us from working as hard as we know we can. While it is certainly true that all of us have limits, Christians constantly ask themselves whether or not they have done everything that God has placed in their power to do. In Paul's second letter to Timothy, he reminded Timothy about doing his best to ensure that his life and doctrine were right. We see this in 2 Timothy 2:14-16:

14 Keep reminding God's people of these things. Warn them before God against quarreling about words; it is of no value, and only ruins those who listen. **15** Do your best to present yourself to God as one approved, a worker who does not need to be ashamed and who correctly handles the word of truth. **16** Avoid godless chatter, because those who indulge in it will become more and more ungodly.
NIV

This admonition to do your best was meant to encourage all of us to strive towards correctly handling God's word with our very best effort. Timothy was the leader of his church, and yet he needed this admonition. How much more do each of us need to be reminded of this? Failure to follow this example will result in our becoming more and more ungodly.

Sometimes, disagreement on spiritual doctrine can be a factor that causes strife within a marriage. This failure to harmonize the common doctrine of the marital body can cause unnecessary quarrelling about words, as is mentioned in the scriptures. A Christian marriage must avoid this type of ungodly chatter by harmonizing the doctrinal beliefs within its body.

God's desire is for His people to be proud of their faith. Being in a minority constituency of faithful believers often discourages us and causes us to shrink back from fervently fulfilling God's plan for us. As evidenced from this scripture, God does not want for us to be ashamed. Marriage is a tool that God uses to build our faith and help us feel like we can fight the battles we are called to fight in this world against sin.

When my wife was pregnant with our first child, there was a television show in syndication known as "Seventh Heaven." This television show was themed around the principles of a small town church minister who was trying to raise his family in the modern era. Every episode was intended to teach morals, principles, and techniques for parenting. Every day, my wife and I watched an episode of this television show and discussed the parental situations that occurred. Sometimes we agreed with the way the situations were handled. Sometimes we felt like we had better ideas or approaches. Sometimes we completely disagreed with how the situations were managed. The most important thing about the time we were spending together was the fact that we were uniting ourselves to each other in our discussion of how we planned to parent our children and exposed for us how our doctrinal beliefs shaped these decisions.

These discussions helped us to understand how each other approached parenting philosophies so we could merge our individual views into one. We learned to appreciate the differences in our fundamental thought processes around parenting and how we viewed our influence on our children. Parenting is often difficult because of the time frame in which children often require a response to their actions. This time we spent together helped us to understand and anticipate how each other would likely respond to various situations. Many of these situations on the show surprised us because when you have never been a parent, there are a great many situations that are not likely to occur to you that are possible scenarios with which you may need to wrestle or manage.

Spending time together discussing how to parent children is vitally important to the success of every married couple with children or couples that plan to have children. A unified couple that understands how they have agreed with one another to parent their children is better able to teach their children in a consistent and intelligible way. Children very quickly learn to play one parent against the other when they are not united with each other. Deep, thorough, and frequent conversations about parenting beliefs and objectives are necessary in order to provide a nurturing and spiritual environment in which children can flourish.

With our first child, we quickly sought advice on how to discipline our son and how early to start. We went to parenting devotionals at our church and quickly learned that the sooner you start a regiment the better when it comes to disciplining and that they are never too young to understand when to obey their parents. This allowed for us to establish a standard of obedience in our home that continues to guide us in raising our children.

Children are not the only ones who profit from parents uniting themselves in their parenting beliefs. Parenting beliefs are a very important subset of how couples need to be united in their spiritual walk together. Upon marriage, few couples agree entirely on how they would like for their children to be raised. In that context, fewer couples still talk in great detail about how they would like for each other to teach their children through specific doctrinal situations and circumstances. Obviously, it will not be possible to predict or anticipate every possible parenting situation that can or will occur. The point in discussing the doctrinal beliefs is to teach each other your preferences and establish some ground rules on your expectations of each other. It also teaches you to understand and anticipate how each other might think about unforeseen or unexpected situations.

Unified parenting starts with a unified foundation of scriptural beliefs. Once a couple has read through the

Bible together and agreed upon its meaning for their lives, this must be the framework from within which they can formulate their parenting beliefs and strategies. Solomon advised of this in Psalm 127:1-2:

> ¹ Unless the LORD builds the house, the builders labor in vain. Unless the LORD watches over the city, the guards stand watch in vain. ² In vain you rise early and stay up late, toiling for food to eat— for he grants sleep to those he loves. **NIV**

This scripture teaches us that if we do not start building our family with our focus solely on God, then our efforts to establish our house is in vain. It also demonstrates how important it is to seek good spiritual guidance to ensure that a proper foundation in being laid.

Much like anything in life, it is always best to get help and guidance from someone that has experience in and knowledge about the area in life in which you are trying to grow or succeed. Solomon expands on this concept in Proverbs 24:3-6:

> ³ By wisdom a house is built, and through understanding it is established; ⁴ through knowledge its rooms are filled   with rare and beautiful treasures. ⁵ The wise

> prevail through great power, and
> those who have knowledge muster
> their strength. ⁶ Surely you need
> guidance to wage war, and victory
> is won through many advisers.
>
> **NIV**

Spiritual men and women seek the counsel of other spiritual men and women who have more or different experience and wisdom. This is best done by studying the Bible with people whose lives you have come to respect. The most influential advice is the advice of someone that you personally know and have witnessed the outcome of his or her way of life. The letter to the Hebrews talks about the way this kind of relationship should bear out in Hebrews 13:7-8:

> ⁷ Remember your leaders, who
> spoke the word of God to you.
> Consider the outcome of their way
> of life and imitate their faith.
> ⁸ Jesus Christ is the same
> yesterday and today and forever.
>
> **NIV**

The Bible is the most effective tool for affecting change in your life and helping you to grow in your capacity to apply God's principles to your life. We can draw comfort from the fact that Jesus does not change and that we can still draw strength from his word and guidance today, just as His followers did thousands of years ago.

Not all church leaders are created equal. Invariably, there will be church leaders whose lives do not resemble the Godly success that you envision through your personal Biblical convictions established within your marital household. Typically, this is due to the fact that all church leaders are still sinners and have not yet attained perfection. While this should not dissuade you from seeking advice, God has given you this discernment so you can consciously consider the outcome of a leader's way of life and determine for yourself what areas in which they excel and how you may learn from the leaders that are closest to you. If you are growing as God intended, it should not surprise you if in order for you to continue growing, it is necessary for you to find a new fellowship of leaders from whom you may further grow and learn.

An important part of understanding this scripture in Hebrews involves paying attention to what it does not say. This scripture calls us to examine the lives of our leaders and imitate their faith. This does not necessarily mean that we should do exactly as they do. On many occasions, we have seen the things that our leaders have done and recognized that their actions required great faith, but we surely would not like to repeat those actions in our own lives. Often times, we have seen leaders do things that were hurtful not only to themselves, but to others around them. While these actions may require great faith, they are not necessarily actions that should be imitated by others. God wants for us to live lives that require great faith while paying careful attention to the outcome of the lives of our leaders.

Establishing a one flesh doctrine is crucial to establishing a functional mechanism through which your relationship can grow. There are a number of scriptures that illustrate this point in various ways. In Deuteronomy 22:9-11, we find:

> [9] Do not plant two kinds of seed in your vineyard; if you do, not only the crops you plant but also the fruit of the vineyard will be defiled. [10] Do not plow with an ox and a donkey yoked together. [11] Do not wear clothes of wool and linen woven together. **NIV**

This scripture is specifically talking about Jewish law. It also has practical application in life because it illustrates how things actually work properly in the spiritual realm. Technically, it may be possible to yoke an ox and a donkey together. However, this would never be the most productive way to plow your field or pull your wagon. A Godly marriage functions in much the same way as these. An unevenly yoked relationship may not immediately kill a marriage, but it will most certainly render it inefficient in executing God's will. In many of these cases, the service rendered may never be worthy of the great God whom we wish to serve.

God has given us the freedom to work out our marriages in many ways. This freedom does not change the fact that living a marital life in accordance with what God has laid out for us in the Bible is the best and most fulfilling way that we can ever hope to live our lives. Some people find themselves content to make a living off of the refuse of their neighbors. This choice to live off of the refuse of others is not typically the will or desire of God for His people. Unfortunately, the reality is that humans, as a species, often settle for much less in life than with what God would truly like to bless them.

Establishing one marital doctrine of beliefs should be a persistent journey of studying God's scriptures. At times, these studies should be done together. At times, these studies should be done separately. Some tough and challenging character studies will often require that a couple spend time with an older or more experienced Christian that can guide them along a specific path. These studies should always result in marital discussions with your spouse to ensure that each person is learning things that are appropriate and as accurate as each member in the marriage can understand.

The foundation of your faith is vitally important to its long term sustenance. For the Christian, this

foundation is the Word of God. Once this foundation is
laid, care must be taken to ensure that a proper and
functioning building is erected upon it. Paul gives some
guidance on this in his first letter to the Corinthian church.
In 1 Corinthians 3:4-15, we find:

> [4] For when one says, "I follow
> Paul," and another, "I follow
> Apollos," are you not mere human
> beings? [5] What, after all, is
> Apollos? And what is Paul? Only
> servants, through whom you came
> to believe —as the Lord has
> assigned to each his task. [6] I
> planted the seed, Apollos watered
> it, but God has been making it
> grow. [7] So neither the one who
> plants nor the one who waters is
> anything, but only God, who makes
> things grow. [8] The one who plants
> and the one who waters have one
> purpose, and they will each be
> rewarded according to their own
> labor. [9] For we are co-workers in
> God's service; you are God's field,
> God's building. [10] By the grace God
> has given me, I laid a foundation
> as a wise builder, and someone
> else is building on it. But each one
> should build with care. [11] For no
> one can lay any foundation other
> than the one already laid, which is

> Jesus Christ. [12] If anyone builds
> on this foundation using gold,
> silver, costly stones, wood, hay or
> straw, [13] their work will be shown
> for what it is, because the Day will
> bring it to light. It will be revealed
> with fire, and the fire will test the
> quality of each person's work. [14] If
> what has been built survives, the
> builder will receive a reward.[15] If it
> is burned up, the builder will suffer
> loss but yet will be saved—even
> though only as one escaping
> through the flames.   **NIV**

Sometimes, Christians get lazy in their faith and, rather
than relying upon God's word to give them direction, they
follow solely the words of mere men. This has become a
common theme within many large church movements.
While it is unlikely that any of the church leaders originally
set out with a sinister plan to lure unsuspecting followers
into a massive movement following them and only them,
this is a reality that has come upon us in many cases. In
fact, many times we have heard people say things like "I
follow Billy Graham" or others. These church leaders are
often in some way victims of their own popularity.
However, it is the responsibility of each individual to
refuse to be held hostage to a denomination or sect due to
its leadership or charismatic speaker.

Perhaps the most important point that Paul is making in this scripture is the importance of spiritual growth. At times, my wife and I have found ourselves in situations where we felt as though we had enjoyable responsibilities in our church, but could not see any measurable growth in our spiritual walk with God. This caused us great concern. In every case, we found ourselves seeking new Christian fellowships that would challenge us by giving us new and different expectations. In some cases, this meant packing up our family and relocating to a church that needed us. Each of us needs to constantly examine ourselves and honestly ask whether or not our fruits of the spirit are more evident this year than last year. Day-to-day fluctuations may not be helpful in your analysis. An honest friend should be able to clearly articulate the growth that they see in you. If this is not the case, then something is not right in your walk with God and you need to seriously contemplate what the best way is for you to make real changes in your spiritual life.

Paul is making an important point to the Corinthians here, helping them to see that neither the church leader nor the well-known book writer is anything of importance at all. God is the one that makes things grow. Quite possibly the single most important thing that a Christian can do is to have their own faith that is separate and apart from any particular church leader, sect, or denomination.

Once you establish and build a faith for yourself, everyone will be able to see the quality of the work you have done. As Paul writes in this passage, your work will be refined by fire. If you expended jewels and costly efforts or sacrifices in order to build your faith, then the quality of your work will be shown for what it is in the time of testing. If you build with poor materials, this will be made known to the world in times of testing as well.

This passage of scripture is meant to impress upon us the importance of laying a solid spiritual foundation and building upon it with real effort. Establishing a one flesh doctrine with your spouse is seldom an easy task, but it is vitally important if you are to survive the testing by fire that awaits you. When building your faith together, be sure to make ample preparation for the ways in which God will use the structure you are building. Spare no expense on this structure because when the storms of life come, it will be the only place in which you can live.

Choosing to do just enough to get by is never an acceptable way to approach serving the God that created the universe. Paul cautions spiritual leaders in this passage in 1 Corinthians by saying that if spiritual leaders are teaching there are limits to what people should do in their service to God, then those leaders may barely survive, but those that they have taught will perish. In truth, it is up to each individual to assess their own personal capabilities of servitude to God. It is our responsibility to have an intimate relationship with God in which we communicate, learn, and grow on a daily basis. Only through this relationship can each individual know what God has called upon them to do on this earth.

Building a marriage that is fulfilling in every way God meant for it to fulfill you requires that you live according to His word. In the Bible, God gives us many examples of the personal sacrifice that He expects and deserves from us. The Bible is not a book of suggestions. God has a plan for our lives and we need to embrace this plan in order for us to have a fulfilling marriage.

Love one another

The Bible offers the most complete definition of love available. In 1 Corinthians 13:1-8 a great example of how to demonstrate your love for your spouse is provided:

> [1] If I speak in the languages of men or of angels, but do not have love, I am only a resounding gong or a clanging cymbal. [2] If I have the gift of prophecy and can fathom all mysteries and all knowledge, and if I have a faith that can move mountains, but do not have love, I am nothing. [3] If I give all I possess to the poor and give over my body to the flames, but do not have love, I gain nothing. [4] Love is patient, love is kind. It does not envy, it does not boast, it is not proud. [5] It does not dishonor others, it is not self-seeking, it is not easily angered, it keeps no record of wrongs. [6] Love does not delight in evil but rejoices with the truth. [7] It always protects, always trusts, always hopes, always perseveres. [8] Love never fails. But where there are prophecies, they will cease; where there are tongues, they will be stilled; where there is knowledge, it will pass away.   **NIV**

This passage of scripture begins by setting up priorities for where love should be in the life of a Christian, comparing love to various other spiritual gifts. Love is exalted here to the highest position amongst all other spiritual gifts because the capacity to express pure love is a truly remarkable gift. After establishing hierarchy, this passage helps us to understand the many personifications of love.

As we can see from this scripture, love is patient, but it is important to understand why it is patient in order to understand how and why we must practice patience. In Matthew 6:14-16, we find:

> [14] For if you forgive other people when they sin against you, your heavenly Father will also forgive you. [15] But if you do not forgive others their sins, your Father will not forgive your sins.   **NIV**

True patience is the natural expression of gratitude for the unlimited patience that God has shown to you. Despite your many shortcomings and failures, God has still seen fit to forgive you. Patience is only ever possible when you have a true and honest view of yourself and your own sin condition. Without a true appreciation of the penalty that you deserve for your sin and how your sin affects God, it is impossible to be truly full of patience for your fellow man or woman. Patience begins with humility and a contrite heart that is consciously aware of its sin.

Love does not envy. Envy is the meaningless pursuit of more than what you already have today. King Solomon expressed his view of envy quite succinctly in Ecclesiastes 4:4:

> [4] And I saw that all toil and all achievement spring from one person's envy of another. This too is meaningless, a chasing after the wind. **NIV**

Envy is vain toil for meaningless achievement. Envy is vain because there will always be more and different things to be had of anything and everything. The endless pursuit of more necessarily displaces the selfless pursuit of the dreams of someone else. Envy is always an expression of selfishness. On the contrary, love is the selfless pursuit of honoring someone else above yourself, pursuing the fulfillment of his or her dreams instead of the fulfillment of your own. Parents often express this part of love naturally for their children, but it is God's call for us to love more than just our children.

Love does not boast because it is not proud. Love is full of humility. Boasting is a failure to grasp the true position of a man or woman. God gives us an example of our true and rightful place in the universe in this text from Jeremiah 18:1-5:

¹ This is the word that came to Jeremiah from the LORD: ² "Go down to the potter's house, and there I will give you my message." ³ So I went down to the potter's house, and I saw him working at the wheel. ⁴ But the pot he was shaping from the clay was marred in his hands; so the potter formed it into another pot, shaping it as seemed best to him. ⁵ Then the word of the LORD came to me. ⁶ He said, "Can I not do with you, Israel, as this potter does?" declares the LORD. "Like clay in the hand of the potter, so are you in my hand, Israel. **NIV**

Boasting is an unrealistic exultation of human importance. The creator of the universe is infinitely superior in power and stature to all men and women. In God's eyes, we are nothing more than clay in the hands of the potter to do with as He wills. In search of the establishment of our own self-importance, we can fall into the trap of boasting about who we are, what we have, or what we have done. In the end, all efforts of mortal man pale in comparison to the Creator. Before our God, we all stand equal. No one is superior to another. The failure to grasp that all of mankind will share the same fate clouds judgment and prevents the true appreciation of others.

Love is the act of placing the interests of someone else ahead of your own interests. Love is not and cannot be self-seeking. This part of love is described in Philippians 2:1-4:

> ¹ Therefore if you have any encouragement from being united with Christ, if any comfort from his love, if any common sharing in the Spirit, if any tenderness and compassion, ² then make my joy complete by being like-minded, having the same love, being one in spirit and of one mind. ³ Do nothing out of selfish ambition or vain conceit. Rather, in humility value others above yourselves,
> ⁴ not looking to your own interests but each of you to the interests of the others. **NIV**

Love, in marriage or otherwise, requires a like-minded commitment to another person. In fact, it is impossible to look to the interests of others without first being aware of what the interests of others may be. Once you know the interests of others, you must value those interests more highly than you value your own interests. This requires trust in God that you will find your own fulfillment without having a need to pursue it on your own. In a marriage, when both spouses seek to fulfill the needs and dreams of the other, something truly beautiful happens. Even when only one marital partner is committed to loving their spouse, a marriage can flourish immensely. The married couple must always strive to be one in spirit and mind.

I remember when my husband and I were dating and had our first really long talk. We discussed the names we wanted to give to our children. From that day forwards, we knew the names of both our children and never looked back. However, in 2003, four years before our first child was born, my father passed away. As daddy's little girl, I had a very close relationship with my father and missed him dearly. After his passing, my husband willingly and graciously offered to name our son after my father. That act of selflessness moved me beyond belief and truly showed how much I meant to my husband that he would be so easily willing to give up a name he had desired in his heart for his very own flesh and blood. This example showed me what true love is all about.

At times, you will need to ask yourself what it means to value others above yourself. In my professional career, I have been fortunate enough to rub elbows with top level executives at some of the largest corporations in the United States. I recall having a conversation once with a friend of mine that was a director of a company. He had spent a lot of time working on a project before a new vice president was hired above him. The new vice president told him to stop working on his project and instead work on some other project that was more important to him. Sometime later, the executive vice president found out about this change and asked the vice president to place the director back on his original project. The vice president then approached the director and told him that he misunderstood him because he never wanted for him to stop working on his original project. In response, the director politely apologized for not paying close enough attention and misunderstanding the direction that was given to him. Although the director was not a Christian (as evidenced by the profanity laced tirade in which he relayed this story to me,) it is clear to me he understands what it means to value someone else above himself. I cannot say that I know very many Christians that would have responded to this situation with the kind of humility and patience he showed, accepting full responsibility for a mistake he had full knowledge that he never actually made.

In a marriage, it is very important to value your spouse more highly than yourself. Imagine a scenario in which your spouse asks you to do 'A'. You actually do 'A'. Your spouse later comes back to you and says "Why did you do 'A'? You misunderstood me, I wanted for you to do 'B'!" In response, you humbly apologize for your mistake (it is your mistake now that you have owned up to it) and make the situation right, while having no bad attitude about the situation whatsoever. If both spouses take this position and practice it regularly, their marriage will become a beautiful thing.

Putting your spouse above yourself is what every Christian is called to do. As we have already seen in 1 Corinthians 6:7, we are called upon to take the position that it is better to be wronged than to propagate disputes. True Christians are not quarrelsome because they have the humility to prefer being wronged to being right and arguing their case.

Love is not easily angered because it freely forgives. To some extent, most people are willing to forgive some things. However, Godly forgiveness is without limits. In Luke 17:1-4, Jesus offered an example for his disciples:

> [1] Jesus said to his disciples: "Things that cause people to stumble are bound to come, but woe to anyone through whom they come. [2] It would be better for them to be thrown into the sea with a millstone tied around their neck than to cause one of these little ones to stumble. [3] So watch yourselves. "If your brother or sister sins against you, rebuke them; and if they repent, forgive them. [4] Even if they sin against

> you seven times in a day and
> seven times come back to you
> saying 'I repent,' you must forgive
> them." **NIV**

True love is the love of someone that is not angered even when someone repeatedly sins against them several times within the same day as in Jesus' example. This is very important in a marriage because within the context of a marriage, two people share an intimate proximity with another sinner in the form of their spouse. Since both members of the union are necessarily sinners, it should be understood and expected that during the course of each day, each spouse will sin against the other. Both spouses desperately need the forgiveness of the other on a consistent basis.

Anger must be avoided because it can invite the devil into your relationship, as it is described in Ephesians 4:25-27:

> [25] Therefore each of you must put
> off falsehood and speak truthfully
> to your neighbor, for we are all
> members of one body. [26] "In your
> anger do not sin": Do not let the
> sun go down while you are still
> angry, [27] and do not give the devil
> a foothold. **NIV**

Anger becomes sin when it is not dealt with and resolved. This sin then further impedes your relationships because the devil can use this sin to gain a foothold in your life and make you an agent of his work. This is why the scripture advises us to urgently address the sin in your life and not allow for it to see the light of another day. The more time you allow for this sin to fester in your heart, the more damage it can do to your soul.

Love does not delight in evil. When a friend or coworker tells an off color joke, laughing is not a loving response. Sin begins to take root in our hearts with the little things and then progresses through us like gangrene. This process is described in James 2:13-15:

> [13] When tempted, no one should say, "God is tempting me." For God cannot be tempted by evil, nor does he tempt anyone; [14] but each person is tempted when they are dragged away by their own evil desire and enticed. [15]Then, after desire has conceived, it gives birth to sin; and sin, when it is full-grown, gives birth to death.
>
> **NIV**

In many ways, sin is like a living parasite. If allowed, it will attach itself to a host organism, feeding off of it until all of the resources and life of the host organism are consumed and both the host and the parasite die. This is why we cannot give sin a foothold in our lives or relationships. The seemingly 'little' sins in our life over time grow up to be 'big' sins that overwhelm and kill us. All sin must be hated in order for love to be genuinely expressed.

Love always protects because it is necessarily consumed with the interest of others. Protection is an active engagement in the concern for another person. Protection cannot wait for a protected person's conscious awareness. An example of this might be a distant military force protecting a nation or standing up for a spouse, when they are not present, and defending their honor and integrity without ever having to make them know that you fought for them. Love is so much more concerned about others than self that it is willing to protect others even from oneself when we are not in a frame of mind to love. This could be the case when you have had a bad day and are prone to being easily angered, you may find that avoiding quick responses can help you put the needs of others above your own and protect them from disparaging fits of rage that might otherwise ensue.

Love always trusts without reservation. This may be one of the most difficult aspects of love because it challenges our self-righteousness. At some time in our lives, all of us have been hurt or disappointed. The natural emotional response that we have been taught is that we should guard our hearts from being hurt or disappointed again. We are taught that we should perhaps withdraw our compassion and hide it so it is not trampled upon once again. Infidelity is one of the most painful violations of trust that a marriage can endure. Some marriages can endure this. Those marriages that survive infidelity can only do so by reestablishing the trust that has been violated. And if not, the two are forever changed and a new marital bond must be formed.

Love always hopes because love is, by definition, the expression of a positive outlook for another person. Hope is actually an ever present thing. Solomon expresses this in Ecclesiastes 9:4:

> ⁴ Anyone who is among the living
> has hope—even a live dog is better
> off than a dead lion!   **NIV**

There is still hope for anyone who is still among the living. As long as they are alive, they have the opportunity to repent and change. When you love someone, you believe the very best things about them. You believe that even though they are human, frail, and sinful, they have the capacity to be great and vibrant people. Love looks beyond what a person is today and sees what he or she can and will be tomorrow.

Marriage is meant to be a permanent relationship. Likewise, true love is also a permanent bond between two people. As we see in 1 Corinthians, love always perseveres no matter what the obstacles may be. With this as the litmus test defining what love actually is, it is not surprising to find that relationships we flippantly call loving relationships, are actually not loving relationships at all. Many relationships purporting to be loving actually fail to persevere through some of the most benign challenges. Marriage vows have been broken over some of the slightest offenses. Contrarily, Ethel Lina White has been quoted as saying "lost causes are the only causes worth fighting for" (The Wheel Spins, 1932, p. 270.) While this quote initially sounds a bit peculiar, it is necessarily what happens when two people love one another. The persistent imperfections of mankind exist within all of us and in some ways make us appear to be a lost cause. Since all of us are sinners and have never achieved perfection, it would appear on the surface that persevering through a relationship with a persistent sinner is a lost cause. God has called upon us to instead put our hope in Him rather than our spouse.

No one is free from the fact that, despite our best efforts, we will always fail our spouse in some way(s). Trying to change or correct your spouse is madness. Your spouse will change when they are ready or able to do so. Love must persevere no matter the outcome because it should be assumed from the beginning that no man or woman has control over changing his or her spouse. Only God can control this. When God is ready to change your spouse for better or for worse, then and only then will your spouse change. God will work on your spouse in ways that will challenge, inspire, and encourage you in ways you never thought possible. To help put this in perspective, let us consider Hebrews 12:4-13:

> [4] In your struggle against sin, you have not yet resisted to the point of shedding your blood. [5] And have you completely forgotten this word of encouragement that addresses you as a father addresses his son? It says, "My son, do not make light of the Lord's discipline, and do not lose heart when he rebukes you, [6] because the Lord disciplines the one he loves, and he chastens everyone he accepts as his son." [7] Endure hardship as discipline; God is treating you as his children. For what children are not disciplined by their father? [8] If you are not disciplined—and everyone undergoes discipline—then you are not legitimate, not true sons and daughters at all. [9] Moreover, we have all had human fathers who disciplined us and we respected them for it. How much more should we submit to the Father of spirits and live![10] They disciplined us for a little while as they thought best;

> but God disciplines us for our good,
> in order that we may share in his
> holiness. [11] No discipline seems
> pleasant at the time, but painful.
> Later on, however, it produces a
> harvest of righteousness and peace
> for those who have been trained by
> it. [12] Therefore, strengthen your
> feeble arms and weak knees.
> [13] "Make level paths for your
> feet," so that the lame may not be
> disabled, but rather healed.
>
> **NIV**

God has promised that He will discipline us for our betterment. This means that He will allow for things that superficially appear to be bad (maybe even horrible) to happen to us to guide us along for His purpose. Anyone that is a child of God will endure things that are intended to make them a better and more useful Christian. We have seen many cases in which the perseverance through the loss of a child or loved one has touched many people and helped them to believe and desire to pursue a closer relationship with God. Being human, we would never wish the loss of a loved one upon anyone. But this is really because we do not see the big picture like God does. God can see not only how this affects people in the immediate short term, but also how it affects His people in the long term course of history.

Love never fails. As in our struggle against sin, we are often guilty of not loving to the point of shedding our blood. True love is love that would surrender one life for another. You should ask yourself this question "If cutting off one or both of my appendages were what my spouse needed for me to do in order that they might better appreciate me, would I do it?" While love is seldom about life or death situations, true love is about whether or not you are willing to make great sacrifices in order that you might place your spouse's desires and needs ahead of your own. If your spouse were going to die if you did not make a given sacrifice, few would be so heartless as to withhold this gift. The never failing love of day-to-day existence is a love that makes great and inconvenient sacrifices in order to sustain even the most mundane desire of their spouse.

Movies and pop culture would have you believe that love is a nothing more than a chance encounter that happens at first sight. This emotional or perhaps even hormonal type of love is not at all what is described or defined in the Bible. It is for this reason that so many people engage in relationships with a wrong and skewed view of what love is or was meant to be. Fortunately, this view can be corrected. The deep appreciation of another person required in order to love them sincerely as called for in the Bible is something that takes time to develop and cultivate. No one loves like this without expending great effort to learn from and listen to his or her spouse.

Only God alone can guide an individual in this matter. The efforts of man alone will always fall short, but the marriage with Christ at its center can mount this challenge and learn to love deeply and sincerely.

The most important part of loving as God has called us to love is growing in our capacity and ability to love. The road that has been marked out ahead of us is one that gets steeper the further we go along. This is not intended to cause us despair, but rather it is there in order that we might always rely on God. It is there so that we might always see our need to expend more efforts. It is there so that we might never feel as if we have arrived at some mystical level of loving and therefore lose our intensity of focus. Paul talks about this in Philippians 3:12-14:

> [12] Not that I have already obtained all this, or have already arrived at my goal, but I press on to take hold of that for which Christ Jesus took hold of me. [13] Brothers and sisters, I do not consider myself yet to have taken hold of it. But one thing I do: Forgetting what is behind and straining toward what is ahead, [14] I press on toward the goal to win the prize for which God has called me heavenward in Christ Jesus. **NIV**

Paul, being the author of more than half of the New Testament, realized that there will be no arrival at your destination while you are here on earth. There will continue to be room for improvement and refining throughout everyone's life. There will never be a time in your marriage when your love for each other can be taken for granted.

There is a popular myth that the honeymoon portion of a marriage is the best time ever experienced in a marriage. People who believe this myth obviously do not believe in this scripture, or they simply do not live their lives in accordance with it. Christians are called to constantly strive for higher goals and objectives. Wherever you are in your walk with God right now, you should be in a better place tomorrow. If you are doing great and wonderful things to serve God and spread His Gospel, then even greater things still await you in the future if you are living in accordance with God's will and plan for your life.

A marriage is a relationship that in many ways bears similarities to other types of interpersonal relationships in that over time, it can and will change or evolve. Whether or not it changes or evolves for the better or worse is largely a function of the decisions made by the participants within the relationship. Christian couples that choose to be obedient to God's word will see to it that they forget what is behind them and press on to ensure their marriage is increasingly more fulfilling as their marriage progresses along.

One of the most dysfunctional expressions of love in marital relationships is the expression of sexuality. Sexuality has been shamefully misused and horribly misunderstood in this world for many centuries. Paul addresses some of the issues that may arise in the sexual conduct of a marriage in 1 Corinthians 7:1-5:

> [1] Now for the matters you wrote about: "It is good for a man not to have sexual relations with a woman." [2] But since sexual immorality is occurring, each man should have sexual relations with his own wife, and each woman with her own husband. [3] The husband should fulfill his marital duty to his wife, and likewise the wife to her husband. [4] The wife does not have authority over her own body but yields it to her husband. In the same way, the husband does not have authority over his own body but yields it to his wife. [5] Do not deprive each other except perhaps by mutual consent and for a time, so that you may devote yourselves to prayer. Then come together again so that Satan will not tempt

you because of your lack of self-
control. **NIV**

While this passage is very complex and has a great deal of
meaning to it, it is very important that we take some time
to understand it. Over the years, we have counseled many
couples on the sexuality in their marriages because
problems in this area of marriage are unfortunately
prevalent.

The failure to have sexual intercourse in a marriage
can be the product of a number of very different things. In
some cases, it may be the result of a spouse's feeling that
having sex is dirty and disgusting. In other cases, strife
within the marriage may cause one or both spouses to feel
like they are no longer physically attracted to each other.
There is no shortage of reasons that may cause and
prolong this problem. However, this passage is clear in its
command that the husband and wife must fulfill their
marital duty to one another or they will suffer the
consequence of Satan's temptation. This scripture is a
warning that should not be taken lightly. The couple that
believes they have so much self-control that they willingly
take on Satan's temptation is foolish beyond reason.

There is room for variance in how a couple can
fulfill their marital duty to one another and still honor God
by obeying this command. Learning to communicate well
is vitally important to making sure that you are meeting

the needs of your spouse. Communication in this area needs to be frequent, detailed, and specific. Marital needs in one month may not even remotely resemble the marital needs in another month. In the span of a lifetime commitment, the fulfillment of marital duty is likely to experience a significant amount of variance over time.

It is not by mistake that Paul advises that spouses do not deprive each other from marital relations except "perhaps" by mutual consent. This is a key point that is sometimes overlooked in marital relationships. Paul is not condoning that couples should ever deprive each other from sexual relations. He is only leaving room for the possibility that in some extreme situations, "perhaps" a couple may deprive each other from sexual relations if and only if they mutually consent to undergo such deprivation. He then goes on to immediately follow this statement with the admonition that during this time of deprivation, you must devote yourselves to prayer and then later come together so that Satan may not tempt you.

We have heard many reasons for couples to not have sexual relations with one another. Most commonly, one spouse is controlling the deprivation and withholding sexual relations from the other. To their shame, they violate this command that Paul has given by failing to acknowledge that their body is not their own. When a couple is one flesh, they surrender their body to their spouse. The husband does not control his body and likewise, the wife does not control her body.

One of the most dangerous reasons we have seen for depriving a spouse of sexual relations is the belief that a spouse is too spiritual or committed to their relationship to stray from their marital bed in thought or deed. This single-sided decision that your spouse is somehow above or beyond temptation is reckless and dangerous. An early example of this is given to us in Genesis 39:1-6a:

> [1] Now Joseph had been taken down to Egypt. Potiphar, an Egyptian who was one of Pharaoh's officials, the captain of the guard, bought him from the Ishmaelites who had taken him there. [2] The LORD was with Joseph so that he prospered, and he lived in the house of his Egyptian master. [3] When his master saw that the LORD was with him and that the LORD gave him success in everything he did, [4] Joseph found favor in his eyes and became his attendant. Potiphar put him in charge of his household, and he entrusted to his care everything he owned. [5] From the time he put him in charge of his household and of all that he owned, the LORD blessed the household of the Egyptian because

> of Joseph. The blessing of the
> LORD was on everything Potiphar
> had, both in the house and in the
> field. **6** So Potiphar left everything
> he had in Joseph's care; with
> Joseph in charge, he did not
> concern himself with anything
> except the food he ate.   **NIV**

To his shame, Potiphar became such a believer in his
invincibility that he found himself concerned only about
the food he ate. At no point was he concerned for the
well-being of his wife. In failing to meet her needs, he
neglected her to the point that she sought the affection of
another man, hoping that maybe with him she might find
the love, affection, and appreciation that she was not
receiving from her husband. This is precisely the kind of
marital deprivation that Paul is advising Christians against
in 1 Corinthians 7. Clearly, Potiphar's wife had not
mutually agreed to this deprivation of marital fulfillment.
As we can see, the nature of Potiphar's occupation, being
the captain of Pharaoh's guard would necessarily mean he
would on occasion be away from his home for long periods
of time. Nevertheless, if his wife has not agreed to this
deprivation of marital duty, then as a Christian, he would
be in no position to hold this occupation as his body is not
his own, but rather belongs to his wife in accordance with
the scriptures.

In our years of counseling married couples, we have seen numerous occasions of this poor and misguided judgment. We have seen pairs of couples leading in various capacities in the church that over time found the spouse of the other couple in leadership more attractive than their own. All too often, this has resulted in two broken marriages and at times, a new marriage has been spawned as a result of the first two marital failures.

Marital duty is a topic from which many couples unfortunately run and yet it has the potential to define, fulfill, or destroy a marriage. Under the guise of freedom, some couples have chosen to minimize their sexual contact. Sometimes this is agreed upon because of mutual desires and sometimes this is agreed upon because couples fear talking about this subject in detail. As a minimum, we recommend that couples fulfill their marital duty to one another at least twice per week. Some couples will be more comfortable with a daily routine, but for most couples, less than twice per week is likely to threaten their intimacy and invite Satan's temptation.

Over time, the fulfillment of marital duty should become more fulfilling and pleasing to a healthy marriage. On the contrary, a couple that has been married for ten years or more and is uncomfortable purchasing lingerie or massaging their spouse is probably a couple with a very confused and dangerously dysfunctional sexual relationship. These things may not be a part of your relationship with your spouse, but they certainly should not make you feel uncomfortable. If the only reason you are fulfilling your marital duty to your spouse is because God has commanded you to do so, then there are likely some serious problems within your relationship that need to be addressed. If you are not familiar with the physical nature of what things should go on in your marriage, then you should seek some help immediately.

Intimacy is a blessing that God desires for every married couple to possess. Solomon talks about this in Proverbs 5:18-19:

> [18] May your fountain be blessed, and may you rejoice in the wife of your youth. [19] A loving doe, a graceful deer— may her breasts satisfy you always, may you ever be intoxicated with her love.
>
> **NIV**

As we grow old together in marriage, we should always be intoxicated by the love of our spouse and our intimacy should always provide us with fulfillment. Newlywed couples often have a degree of intimacy, but couples that have been married for longer periods of time should have learned through great struggles how to find fulfillment, enjoyment, and intoxication from the intimate relationship they share with their spouse.

Early in our marriage, my wife and I had some arguments that ended very badly for both of us. A couple of these arguments resulted in my wife getting into her car and leaving. Having less than two years invested in our marriage at this time, I was perfectly content to let her go and never return if that were her choice. In retrospect, this shows me that although I loved my wife, in the early stages of our marriage we still had tenuous ties that bound the two of us together. Building a solid relationship that goes beyond the emotional highs and lows of life takes time and a great deal of effort. God loves us and freely provides us with challenges and struggles that will forge a deep and intimate relationship, if we seek His will and listen attentively to the lessons He wants for us to learn in our lives. These challenges are not meant to discourage or dishearten us, but help us to rely upon each other, value each other's skills and insights, and learn to depend upon each other with a trust that only experience can produce.

Now that we have children, finding time to be intimate has become more challenging. However, at the same time, we have also found fulfillment in a variety of ways that do not always include the physical act of expressing our love. Just the other day, my husband made sure we dropped off our children early for babysitting just to give ourselves a little more time together. That act alone was fulfilling, both from the aspect of my husband wanting to spend more time with me and the opportunity to actually do so. The funny thing is that the extra time was spent just driving around and talking to each other about our days.

God's desire for us is that regardless of our current stage in life that we should rejoice in the spouse of our youth. Youth is certainly relative as some people first marry at older ages than others. In all of this, we should rejoice and find fulfillment and satisfaction in our lives on account of this relationship. Perhaps you have outlived your spouse. You should still feel a sense of satisfaction and fulfillment from that relationship because this relationship was created for you for the purpose of fulfilling your needs.

My wife and I have often remarked on how we seem to have virtually nothing in common with one another. I very much enjoy history, while my wife abhors it. She is very much interested in the arts and entertainment, and I have difficulty finding any interest in this at all. In matters of trivia, we have virtually no overlapping bases of knowledge. If we could enter a game show as a team, we might well have everything in the world covered. As we examine this, it becomes clear to us that God has placed us together in our relationship so that we might complete each other. Everything that my wife excels in, I find myself lacking. Everything I excel in, my wife likewise needs me to fill in the gaps. We are a team that God designed for His purposes to do His will and we cannot accomplish His tasks without each other.

Marital fulfillment is a matter of personal choice. The way that you view the differences between yourself and your spouse is also a matter of choice. If you are wise, you will view your spouse's strengths as your own personal strengths on a different part of your body to be used as you need it. If you are foolish, you will look upon your differences as aberrances that must be conformed or competed against. This latter behavior will never produce fulfilling relationships.

There will always be opportunities to desire things that are beyond or different than what God has created for you, but God has purposed that you should be satisfied and fulfilled with the spouse that He has created specifically for you. Failure to make the personal choice of fulfillment in your marriage is rooted in the same greed that causes us to not find fulfillment in our income. In Ecclesiastes 5:10, we find:

> **10** Whoever loves money never has enough; whoever loves wealth is never satisfied with their income. This too is meaningless.
>
> **NIV**

Solomon further explains this concept in Ecclesiastes 3:12-13:

> **12** I know that there is nothing
> better for people than to be happy
> and to do good while they live.
> **13** That each of them may eat and
> drink, and find satisfaction in all
> their toil—this is the gift of God.
>
> **NIV**

Finding satisfaction in our toil of life does not happen without us first searching it out and discovering it through personal sacrifice. In much the same way, we have to seek out our personal satisfaction and fulfillment in our marital relationships. This satisfaction is a gift from God that has been given to us, but many of us never unwrap the gift to recognize the priceless treasure that has been bequeathed to us for our enjoyment and fulfillment. Regardless of how you may feel about your marriage today, you can start to pursue finding fulfillment in your relationship. You will probably need some help on this journey, but that fact should not discourage you. Digging for treasure is hard work, but in the end the returns are priceless.

Get your priorities in order

Building a great marriage as God intended can only be accomplished by seeking first the kingdom of God above everything else. God has established for His people a plan for their lives that goes beyond just having the blessing of a great marriage. The power to build a great marriage is fueled by the desire to align your priorities with God's priorities.

Building a one flesh marriage as God intended it requires that you put the right kind of fuel in your tank. The engine of God's people requires a highly refined fuel of faith and personal effort to grow and express that faith. We call this the "seeking God" fuel. In much the same way that we talked about earlier when discussing God's conditional promises for us, God wants to energize us and give us the strength to build a marriage as He intended it when we seek Him first. The only way for us to get this fuel into our tank is for us to spare no expense of energy and effort to seek first God's kingdom.

Nothing binds a couple together like being unified in the mission of Christ. Christ's mission is the ultimate basis for personal fulfillment in life. A fulfilled life can only come from firmly establishing yourself in the priorities of Christ. Jesus laid out a simple map for priorities in Matthew 6:25-33:

> 25 "Therefore I tell you, do not
> worry about your life, what you will

eat or drink; or about your body, what you will wear. Is not life more than food, and the body more than clothes? **26** Look at the birds of the air; they do not sow or reap or store away in barns, and yet your heavenly Father feeds them. Are you not much more valuable than they? **27** Can any one of you by worrying add a single hour to your life? **28** "And why do you worry about clothes? See how the flowers of the field grow. They do not labor or spin. **29** Yet I tell you that not even Solomon in all his splendor was dressed like one of these. **30** If that is how God clothes the grass of the field, which is here today and tomorrow is thrown into the fire, will he not much more clothe you—you of little faith? **31** So do not worry, saying, 'What shall we eat?' or 'What shall we drink?' or 'What shall we wear?' **32** For the pagans run after all these things, and your heavenly Father knows that you need them. **33** But seek first his kingdom and his righteousness, and all these things will be given to you as well.

NIV

In many ways, it may seem obvious that there is more to life than the basic physical necessities of survival and warmth. However, at the same time, it is often equally easy to fill our lives with endless schemes in the pursuit of improving and maintaining our living conditions. On some level, we are all consciously aware of the fact that worrying about the needs, wants, and concerns of this life can in no way extend our lives. Unfortunately, we sometimes fail to understand what it really means to seek first God's kingdom. Some church groups advocate daily "quiet times" in which you read your Bible for ten minutes every day and pray to God for five minutes. Certainly this is not a bad practice, but is this really putting God first in our lives? Being religious is not necessarily the same thing as placing God first and in the forefront of our lives. To place God first, we must examine our lives carefully and consider whether or not we are giving God our best.

Above all else, the purpose of a married couple is to seek first God's kingdom. God knows that we need toiletries, clothing, and food. Seeking first God's kingdom means that you put forth your very best effort towards being the Christian that God wants for you to be. The most challenging things in your marriage can only be overcome when you put God so far ahead of all of your other priorities that you become a radically changing person every day. The key thing about seeking God first is recognizing that God is a great King and needs to be revered above everything else in your life.

In Malachi 1:12-14, God talks about how He is to be revered among the nations because He is a great king:

> [12] "But you profane it by saying, 'The Lord's table is defiled,' and, 'Its food is contemptible.' [13] And you say, 'What a burden!' and you sniff at it contemptuously," says the LORD Almighty. "When you bring injured, lame or diseased animals and offer them as sacrifices, should I accept them from your hands?" says the LORD. [14] "Cursed is the cheat who has an acceptable male in his flock and vows to give it, but then sacrifices a blemished animal to the Lord. For I am a great king," says the LORD Almighty, "and my name is to be feared among the nations. **NIV**

In this passage, God asks some very pointed questions. When offering your time, energy, and efforts to God, would your employer accept those efforts? Would your spouse accept those efforts from you? God is a great king and as such, He deserves to be given the first and very best efforts that you have to offer. God is not to be offered your leftover time or efforts. Cursed is the cheat who pledges to put God first in their life, but instead devotes all of their free time to advancing their career, job, or hobby.

Seeking first God's kingdom and His righteousness means that nothing short of your best efforts toward seeking God and developing righteousness can be accepted by God. Anything less than our very best effort is a foolish attempt on our part to cheat God out of what is rightfully due Him. God expects and deserves for us to seek a deep and meaningful relationship with Him. This will mean different things for different people. It cannot be measured simply in minutes reading the Bible.

Seeking God involves more than just Bible study and prayer. Seeking God is manifested in our daily lives through our efforts to live out and complete Christ's mission. Jesus summarizes the purpose of His mission in Luke 19:9-10:

> [9] Jesus said to him, "Today salvation has come to this house, because this man, too, is a son of Abraham. [10]For the Son of Man came to seek and to save the lost."
> **NIV**

There is an entire world of people that do not yet know what it means to have a deep and intimate relationship with God. There are people who have no idea what it means to truly put God at the very first place in their lives. This is often not because people have no intention of placing God first, but sadly, some people find themselves lacking the spiritual ambition to do so.

Spiritual ambition starts with clear spiritual vision. Well meaning Christians often struggle with obtaining a vision for how their lives can be better. This is always to the detriment of God's people. This is not a new or modern challenge, but throughout history, people have struggled with not only seeing their sin and addressing it, but also focusing on and executing Jesus' mission of saving this lost world. Jesus addressed the issue of spiritual vision in Matthew 7:1-5:

> [1] "Do not judge, or you too will be judged. [2] For in the same way you judge others, you will be judged, and with the measure you use, it will be measured to you. [3] "Why do you look at the speck of sawdust in your brother's eye and pay no attention to the plank in your own eye? [4] How can you say to your brother, 'Let me take the speck out of your eye,' when all the time there is a plank in your own eye? [5] You hypocrite, first take the plank out of your own eye, and then you will see clearly to remove

the speck from your brother's eye.
NIV

Sadly, people often misunderstand this scripture and come away with the idea that we are not to judge one another (as if that were possible). As humans, we are in our very nature judgmental. However, we are being called in this scripture to address the sin in our lives that prevents us from having spiritual vision. When we have addressed the sin in our own lives, we can then see clearly to judge and remove the speck from our spiritual brother's eye. This metaphor is intended to help us see the importance of dealing with all of the sin in our lives so that we can see clearly and be useful in God's kingdom, as we all know how difficult it is to fumble about when you are not able to see. Likewise, we cannot be helpful to our spouse until we righteously address the speck in our own eye.

Some of the most Biblically knowledgeable people we know are lousy parents and do not love their spouses. We live in a time and place where knowing the Bible can sometimes get confused with the repentance of sin or spiritual growth. In Jesus' time, these people were often called Pharisees. Today, we seldom if ever address these issues in our own lives. Those whom we consider to be "Spiritual" people are often people who do nothing more than come to church, read their Bible, and pray. If seeking first God's kingdom were that simple, probably everyone would be a Christian. God wants and expects our very best. Consider the latter part of Matthew 7 in verses 21-23:

> [21] "Not everyone who says to me, 'Lord, Lord,' will enter the kingdom of heaven, but only the one who does the will of my Father who is in heaven. [22] Many will say to me on that day, 'Lord, Lord, did we not prophesy in your name and in your name drive out demons and in your name perform many miracles?' [23] Then I will tell them plainly, 'I never knew you. Away from me, you evildoers!' **NIV**

Obviously, there will be people that call themselves Christians and perform many miraculous works in Jesus' name that are not going to heaven. What is worse here is that Jesus is saying He never even knew these people. It seems impossible to imagine that these people did not read their Bibles. It seems impossible to imagine that these people did not regularly attend a church. Since they are performing miraculous acts in Jesus' name, it seems impossible to imagine that these people did not pray fervently (perhaps even more fervently than some who are reading this book). Voltaire has been quoted as saying "The perfect is the enemy of the good." His point was that the concepts of good and perfect are diametrically opposed to one another. In our sloth and laziness, our tendency is to consider how much is good enough. For those of us that are unclear on this point, Jesus spells it out for us in no uncertain terms in Matthew 5:48:

> [8] Be perfect, therefore, as your heavenly Father is perfect.
>
> **NIV**

In our quick assessment of this scripture, our natural tendency is to assume that this is some sort of relative marker where if we are better than our neighbor, then we are probably safe. While this scripture probably does only have meaning in a relative sense, the relative comparison is to one's self and not to one's neighbor. The pursuit of spiritual perfection never ends for anyone. God expects for you to give Him your best, not your neighbor's best. Perhaps you are more spiritual than your neighbor will ever be on his best day. You still have room for improvement. Achieving a level that is in some way perceived as being higher than that of another person does not entitle you to end your pursuit of perfection. God has one standard – perfection. At any given point in time, everyone is in a different place in their journey towards achieving that goal. The fact that your neighbor has not laced up his or her boots yet doesn't mean that you have won the race by default. You are not racing against your neighbor, you are racing against yourself. If you don't run like the wind without looking back, you will find yourself in danger of losing the race.

Jesus gives us an illustration of His expectations from us by way of a story He tells in Matthew 7:7-8 & 7:13-14:

> [7] "Ask and it will be given to you; seek and you will find; knock and the door will be opened to you.
> [8] For everyone who asks receives; the one who seeks finds; and to the one who knocks, the door will be opened. **NIV**
> [13] "Enter through the narrow gate. For wide is the gate and broad is the road that leads to destruction, and many enter through it. [14] But small is the gate and narrow the road that leads to life, and only a few find it. **NIV**

Jesus uses these passages to build a clear picture of what it means for someone to seek His kingdom. First, He makes the point that everyone that asks will receive; everyone that seeks will find; everyone that knocks will have the door opened to them. He immediately turns this statement around and seemingly contradicts Himself by challenging His followers to enter through the narrow gate. He argues that there is a narrow gate through which Christians must pass in order to enter into life. The imagery here suggests that with such a narrow road, it would be easy to slip off of the road if the traveler is not attentive or finds themself being careless. One of the more curious parts of this passage is the claim that only a few will find the narrow gate. If in just a few verses earlier, Jesus says that everyone that seeks finds, then it must be true that not everyone is really and truly seeking. These exhortations are meant to paint a picture of the kind of search that God wants from His people.

Once you are able to clearly see your sin, you have to actively engage in repentance. Let us consider some of the direction that Timothy received on selecting leaders in his church. In 1 Timothy 3:1-5 we find:

> [1] Here is a trustworthy saying: Whoever aspires to be an overseer desires a noble task. [2] Now the overseer is to be above reproach, faithful to his wife, temperate, self-controlled, respectable, hospitable, able to teach, [3] not given to drunkenness, not violent but gentle, not quarrelsome, not a lover of money. [4] He must manage his own family well and see that his children obey him, and he must do so in a manner worthy of full respect. [5] (If anyone does not know how to manage his own

family, how can he take care of
God's church?)   **NIV**

A very valid question is raised at the end of this passage. It should be obvious that a spiritual person must be able to manage their own family. Unfortunately, in the United States, there is a rising number of divorced ministers. This is especially unfortunate because the family unit is the spiritual proving ground for God's leaders.

Being above reproach in your marriage means avoiding anything that might be questionable or potentially misunderstood if taken out of context. Simply put, this is perhaps one of the most difficult calls to lay upon a leader. Doing what is right and obeying the letter of God's law that is put before us can eventually become relatively easy with time and training. However, being above reproach goes beyond that and demands not only your intentions be pure, but also your interpretations must be pure. For example, it is not by accident that we do not keep any religious paraphernalia on our motor vehicles. While it would never be our intention to operate our vehicles in a sinful manner, we recognize and take seriously the possibility that we may misrepresent God's people if we inadvertently cut someone off in traffic without noticing them. To be above reproach is to ensure that you never even so much as accidentally misrepresent God's kingdom even out of negligence when you are not consciously aware of it.

Being faithful to your spouse may seem like an elementary thing, but it is a requirement that must be maintained. If God's people are to set an example in this world of how God's plan is meant to be set into action, we must live in such a way that our lives are worthy of respect. Faithfulness to your spouse is a way to demonstrate your love for them. It shows that you are committed despite the fact that each of you will sin against each other over time. Fidelity is an act that is born out of unconditional love.

Simply put, seeking first God's righteousness means dealing with sin and growing in areas of spiritual qualities. Growing in righteousness and repenting of sin are two sides of the same coin of change which God would like to produce in all of us. There are several lists of sin and righteousness found in the Bible. One such list is found in Galatians 5:19-26:

> [19] The acts of the flesh are obvious: sexual immorality, impurity and debauchery; [20] idolatry and witchcraft; hatred, discord, jealousy, fits of rage, selfish ambition, dissensions, factions [21] and envy; drunkenness, orgies, and the like. I warn you, as I did before, that those who live like this will not inherit the kingdom of God. [22] But

> the fruit of the Spirit is love, joy,
> peace, forbearance, kindness,
> goodness, faithfulness,
> [23] gentleness and self-control.
> Against such things there is no
> law. [24] Those who belong to Christ
> Jesus have crucified the flesh with
> its passions and desires. [25] Since
> we live by the Spirit, let us keep in
> step with the Spirit. [26] Let us not
> become conceited, provoking and
> envying each other.   **NIV**

The call here is to repent of the acts of the flesh and excel in the fruit of the Spirit. Despite the obvious nature of these fleshly sins noted, many Christians repent of things they consider to be more obvious and expend little to no effort to repent of things they consider to be less obvious. For example, it would not be right to repent of sexual immorality, but make no effort to repent of envying your neighbors possessions or hating your coworker. Excelling in the fruit of the Spirit requires both focus and effort. No one has ever become self-controlled by accident. Self-control requires discipline and training. Self-control is the foundation for all of the fruits of the Spirit because executing on all of them requires that you first develop self-control so you do not react to situations, but rather respond with appropriate and carefully considered Spiritual responses.

Seeking first God's righteousness means ridding our lives of all acts of the flesh described in Galatians. Furthermore, we must rid ourselves of the appearance of these acts of the flesh. Rightly so, it has oft been said that you may be the only Bible that someone ever reads. This is to say that your example of Spirituality may form someone's entire view of Christianity and be the basis on which someone decides whether or not to become a Christian or seek a relationship with God.

Even if you are not actually engaged in sexual immorality, you must set an example of purity so that no one could even surmise that you might possibly be sexually immoral. This is elaborated upon in Ephesians 5:3-7:

> [3] But among you there must not be even a hint of sexual immorality, or of any kind of impurity, or of greed, because these are improper for God's holy people. [4] Nor should there be obscenity, foolish talk or coarse joking, which are out of place, but rather thanksgiving.
> [5] For of this you can be sure: No immoral, impure or greedy person —such a person is an idolater—has any inheritance in the kingdom of Christ and of God. [6]Let no one deceive you with empty words, for because of such things God's wrath

comes on those who are
disobedient. [7] Therefore do not be
partners with them.   **NIV**

This passage is helpful in terms of understanding the
scripture in Galatians. This scripture makes it clear that
seeking first God's kingdom means that there cannot be
even so much as a hint of sin in our lives because these
things are improper for God's holy people. Seeking first
God's kingdom means that there can be no obscenity in
our lives, either spoken by us or tolerated from others in
our lives.

Some people have asked us "what is coarse
joking?" We generally answer that this as any kind of
joking that makes too light of a serious sinful situation.
Certainly God has a sense of humor and there is room for
responsible joking, but care should be taken. For example,
we once counseled a couple where the wife had a married
female friend in the church with whom she had become
very comfortable after many years of friendship. One
evening, after spending some girl time together, the ladies
came home and the wife and her married friend
pretended to engage in threesome sexual activity with her
husband. Given that both women were members of the
same church, there was no intention that this would get
out of hand, but unfortunately it escalated to the point
where the husband had sex with the wife's friend while
the wife was present in the house. It was at this point that

the wife no longer found the joke to be funny. Fortunately, both couples were able to go before the church, confess their sin and repent. As of the writing of this book, both marriages have survived this unfortunate coarse joke, but both have suffered significant damage to their marriages.

Coarse joking can be a very dangerous and caustic element to a marital relationship. A deep and intimate relationship cannot be built upon glib humor that masks true feelings. Sometimes, coarse joking can be used by couples that are afraid to talk to each other about how they feel in deep and meaningful ways. This "humor" is then used as a way to avoid talking about things that are difficult to hear. All of us sin and at times, we will sin against our spouse. The result of this sin is that we must talk about how the sin makes us feel towards one another. Few of us really want to hear from our spouse how we are imperfect and need to be better people, but we must have these conversations if we are ever going to have deep relationships with each other. Joking and making light of our sinful situations do not help us to be the Christians God wants for us to be.

In our modern times, we often have trouble relating to the concept of idolatry, as we see examples in the Bible of people building golden calves and worshiping these obviously physically created objects as though they were in some way divine. While this may not be the dominant form of idolatry in the world today, the passage in Ephesians 5 extends the definition of idolatry to include immorality, impurity, and greed. Some very strong words are used against such people who fall into this category of idolatry. This passage tells us that no one who is greedy for any kind of personal gain has any inheritance in the kingdom of Christ. This statement seems antithetical to the American way of excessive greed and consumption.

The American way of living has long been a systematic consumption of more than is needed of everything. This attitude has permeated so much of American culture that few Americans have any idea what really and truly constitutes a need and what is a luxury. Even the amount of income that the United States government considers to be "poverty level" of income for one person would place an individual in the top 15% of wage earners in the entire world. The United States' perception of need versus want has been skewed quite significantly. History tells us that this is a momentary problem and American appetites will necessarily be adjusted at some point, but at the writing of this book, the United States of America is in danger of failing to understand what it means to not be greedy. At this present time, greed in America stands tall as the most virtuous of virtues.

Seeking first God's kingdom means that you must
not only avoid and repent of sin in your own life, but you
must also condemn it in the lives of others around you.
The last line in the Ephesians passage tells us that we
cannot be partners with people who are enemies of God,
as described earlier in the text. This would limit our ability
to engage in business activity with all people that do not
live in accordance with God's covenant. Let us consider
the fate of Jehoshaphat, King of Judah, as his story is told
in 2 Kings 3:11-14 and 2 Chronicles 20:35-37:

> **11** But Jehoshaphat asked, "Is
> there no prophet of the LORD here,
> through whom we may inquire of
> the LORD?"   An officer of the king
> of Israel answered, "Elisha son of
> Shaphat is here. He used to pour
> water on the hands of Elijah."
> **12** Jehoshaphat said, "The word of
> the LORD is with him." So the king
> of Israel and Jehoshaphat and the
> king of Edom went down to him.
> **13** Elisha said to the king of Israel,
> "Why do you want to involve me?
> Go to the prophets of your father
> and the prophets of your mother."
> "No," the king of Israel answered,
> "because it was the LORD who
> called us three kings together to
> deliver us into the hands of Moab."
> **14** Elisha said, "As surely as the

LORD Almighty lives, whom I
serve, if I did not have respect for
the presence of Jehoshaphat king
of Judah, I would not pay any
attention to you. **NIV**

35 Later, Jehoshaphat king of Judah
made an alliance with Ahaziah king
of Israel, whose ways were
wicked. 36 He agreed with him to
construct a fleet of trading ships.
After these were built at Ezion
Geber, 37 Eliezer son of Dodavahu
of Mareshah prophesied against
Jehoshaphat, saying, "Because you
have made an alliance with
Ahaziah, the LORD will destroy
what you have made." The ships
were wrecked and were not able to
set sail to trade. **NIV**

Although Jehoshaphat was a righteous man who made
alliances with Ahab and his son Ahaziah, these alliances
with unrighteous men ultimately cost him his life.

In 2 Kings, we see that if it were not for the
righteousness of Jehoshaphat, the prophet Elisha would
not have even spoken to the kings that had summoned
him. King Ahaziah followed in the footsteps of his father
and became a stumbling block to Jehoshaphat because
Jehoshaphat put his trust in the army and navy of Israel
rather than placing his trust in God.

We see this happen many times over as young Christians are fearful of giving up jobs that place them in bad spiritual situations. The decision to put your trust in your income to sustain you over putting your trust in God to sustain you, when you are defying an ungodly situation, never meets with positive results. Christians do not have to be partners with sinners because their lives are not dependent upon it. This is not to say that a Christian can only work for a "Christian" company. All of the successful corporate leaders that we know personally employ many spiritual attributes. None of these people are Christians and few of them even believe in God. However, they are people who have learned through life that God's principles work and they have been blessed in their lives because they live Godly lives though not through Godly motives. These people have learned to be patient, humble, and self-controlled for the purpose of financial gain. Fortunately for them, God's promise of blessings to those who develop these attributes is freely available to all people; regardless of their ultimate spiritual state of salvation.

Seeking first God's kingdom will always involve intense personal sacrifice. While everyone's walk with God is unique and different, the call for each and every one of us to make daily personal sacrifices to seek God is absolutely identical. This call transcends socioeconomic status as well as leadership role within a particular church. It would not be right for a church leader to believe that because they are a leader in God's church they would no longer need to step up their level of sacrifice. God expects and deserves that in our walk with Him. We must constantly push ourselves to our limits and excel in our sacrifice today in a measure that exceeds our level of sacrifice that we achieved yesterday. As Paul said in Philippians 3, we must press on towards the goal, forgetting what is behind us. Yesterday was only good enough for yesterday. Today, God deserves that we soar to heights never seen before by men.

With a sacrificial, God seeking attitude we can attain the marriage that God has intended for us to experience since the beginning of time. Regardless of where you are in your walk with God today, the first priority in your life must be to seek God. If you get this priority on right, then there are no limits to what God can do in your life and the blessings He can bestow upon you. Just like with all of God's blessings, you have to make the first step by going out on faith and seeking Him with all of your heart. God is right there with you eagerly desiring to fill you up with His blessings, if you would only reach out and seek Him.